RESOLVING UNFINISHED BUSINESS

Assessing The Effects of Being Raised In a Dysfunctional Environment

Anthony S. Dallmann-Jones, Ph.D.

Professor
MARIAN COLLEGE

Director
INSTITUTE FOR TRANSFORMATIONAL STUDIES
Fond du Lac, Wisconsin

RESOLVING UNFINISHED BUSINESS
Assessing The Effects of Being Raised In a Dysfunctional Environment

ISBN# - 1-881952-26-6

Author: Anthony S. Dallmann-Jones, Ph.D.

Three Blue Herons Publishing, Inc.
P.O. Box 463
Fond du Lac, WI 54936-0463
414/921-6991
414/921-7691 (Fax)

ACKNOWLEDGEMENTS

Thank you, Steven Farmer, for your insight, assistance, and friendship in putting this work together.

Thank you Charles Whitfield, M.D., and David Chadwick, M.D., for your editorial assistance.

Thank you Terry Kellogg and John Bradshaw for your mind-expanding and heart-opening work, and to Alice Miller, one of the greatest champions children ever had.

Special acknowledgement goes to my dedicated editor and wife, Amy, for her incredible intelligence, skill, patience and–one of the most important qualities in life, work and relationship–sense of humor.

~Dedicated to the Walking Wounded~

Those that continue to suffer the consequences
of being raised in a less than nurturing family.

TABLE OF CONTENTS

Introduction 1

Chapter One
Dysfunctional 7

Chapter Two
Life's Toolbox of Skills and Techniques
An Explanation 11

Chapter Three
Abuse & Neglect and Susceptibility
Human Sensitivity 17
Human Intelligence 18
Human Adaptability 19
Addiction as Adaptation 20

Chapter Four
The Many Forms of Abuse
Towards a Nomenclature of Human
Abuse & Neglect 25
Definition of Abuse & Neglect 27

Chapter Five
The Dysfunctional Family Survivor Syndrome
1) Control Consciousness 31
2) Avoiding Emotions 32
3) Inability to Grieve 32

4) Guilt from Overresponsibility 33
5) Crisis Addiction 33
6) Guessing at Normality 34
7) Low Self-Esteem 34
8) Compulsive Behaviors 35
Limits and Boundaries 35
Recovery. 36

Chapter Six
Implications for RELATIONSHIPS 39

Chapter Seven
Implications for EDUCATION. 51

Chapter Eight
Implications for BUSINESS. 67

Chapter Nine
Why Is Abuse Harmful?. 83
Relationships of Abuse Forms 86

Chapter Ten
Value and Utilization of the CSCAN
The Value of a Nomenclature 89
A Notation and Reporting System of
Abuse & Neglect. 90

Notes on Utilizing the Appendices and Support Groups . 93

Appendix I

The Classification System of Child Abuse & Neglect (CSCAN) 97
Physical Abuse (PA) 99
Physical Neglect (PN) 100
Emotional Abuse (EA). 102
Emotional Neglect (EN) 103
Mental Abuse (MA) 104
Mental Neglect (MN) 106
Sexual Abuse (SA) 107
Sexual Neglect (SN) 108
Vicarious Abuse (VA) 108

Appendix II

Adult Forms of Abuse & Neglect
Adult Abuse/Adult Self-Abuse 111
Adult Physical Self-Abuse (APS-A). 113
Adult Physical Abuse (APA) 114
Adult Mental Self-Abuse (AMS-A) 116
Adult Mental Abuse (AMA) 116
Adult Emotional Self-Abuse (AES-A). 118
Adult Emotional Abuse (AEA) 118
Adult Sexual Self-Abuse (ASS-A) 119
Adult Sexual Abuse (ASA) 120
Adult Financial Self-Abuse(AFS-A) 121
Adult Financial Abuse (AFA) 121

Appendix III
Triangulation
A Common and Complex
Form of Social Abuse 123
Positioning, Maneuvering and Rules in the
Triangle 130
Avoiding the Triangle 134

Appendix IV
Assessment Forms
Family Health Continuum 140
Personal Health Continuum 142

Bibliography 145

Institute for Transformational Studies 149
Mission Statement
Gillette Manor

Products & Order Form. 150

The WINDOORS Program & Training 153

About the Author 154

Index 155

INTRODUCTION

This book is about liberation and power. Knowledge is liberation. Freedom of choice is power. Adult survivors of dysfunctional families were raised in ignorance, and they become shackled by that ignorance—ignorance about emotions, relationships with others and self, limits and boundaries, and other essential tools and skills necessary for a thriving life. This ignorance leaves adult survivors with limited choices and, therefore, limited power. Their universe has been artificially restricted by unenlightened caregivers who, perhaps unintentionally, have constricted to a mere slice what life has to offer them, and what they have to offer life.

To accomplish the quest for full personhood, we must finish our business with our parents and/or caregivers. If we do not, we will, wittingly and unwittingly, project this unfinished business into all our relationships, especially that significant spiritual relationship with ourselves. We have the need and right to be our own person.

This book concentrates almost totally on the effects of abuse within and around the victim. In this book I am not as concerned with blame as I am with the *dynamics* of abuse and neglect, their aftereffects, and how, once started, these dynamics develop an identity of their own. This identity, which I call the Dysfunctional Family Survivor Syndrome, impacts both the victim's life and the lives of those around the victim. The impact of this intra- and interpersonal virus is deadening at best and deadly at worst. It is of such criticality that we understand the dynamics of the long-term effects of abuse and neglect that we must temporarily suspend our concerns of fault-finding, social implications, and litigation issues. In this way we can impartially and objectively see what lies behind the veil of this virulent syndrome.

In our world today, I see a conspiracy to offer more protection for perpetrating adults than for their helpless victims, especially when the abuser is a parent. It is incredible that we still find a children-as-chattel mentality surviving to the detriment of our children's welfare. The goal herein is to disseminate psychodynamic understanding of the consequences of abuse and neglect. With such understanding we can better focus our resources to more effectively champion the children.

There are those who denigrate the need for understanding dysfunctional family survivor dynamics, usually while carefully tending their own symptoms. Some of us wonder what keeps these sister and fellow human beings so blind to their own condition, often appearing righteous in their misery. Some call it arrogance; some call it denial. It is as if they are incapable of seeing the impact of such devastation in their own and other's lives: "Yes, I'm miserable. There may or may not be help, but I'm not going to avail myself of it even if there is." Perhaps this book can help remove the blinders of denial. I can only assure the reader that they have much to gain, namely freedom and power, and little to lose, except for old pain and the fatigue of carrying around heavy and unnecessary baggage that should have been dropped long ago.

Survivors eventually manifest what my colleague Steven Farmer and I have termed the Dysfunctional Family Survivor (DFS) Syndrome. I have dedicated several chapters to exploring the implications of the DFS Syndrome in our relationships, schools, and work places. Within the framework provided by this book's purposes is also a proposed *nomenclature* of abuse and neglect, plus a means of assessing your family of origin during your formative years and yourself now. These provide a good means of internalizing the material. If more in-depth coverage or resources are wanted or needed, the bibliography is a good place to start looking.

There is some unpleasant truth in this book. Fortunately, the flipside of this information is positive empowerment to do something about the burdensome baggage. Internalizing the information in this book can help the individual avoid denial, the carrier of all dysfunctionality, and can facilitate effective self and social intervention in putting an end to what often becomes a vicious cycle of abuse and neglect.

A Note About Attitude and Breathing

Whether you are reading this professionally or personally I urge you to pay attention to your breathing as you read and work through the material. Encourage yourself to keep your breathing circular with a relaxed exhale. Your breathing is an excellent detector of unfinished business. If you reach some places in the material where you feel smothered or unable to breathe deeply, that passage is especially significant for you. Gently remind yourself to "Breathe in a circle with a relaxed exhale" and mark whatever you are reading at that moment. With this easily used breathing and marking technique it should be possible for you to read the whole book without skipping or phasing out on the parts that are probably the most important to you. Since you have to breathe anyway, why not breathe in a manner that benefits you?

Suggestion:
Please read the entire book before doing the self-assessment instruments located in Appendix IV.

CHAPTER ONE

DYSFUNCTIONAL

I don't like the word "dysfunctional" because it sounds like broken or damaged goods. Many think it refers to the most degenerative of families, but actually it applies in some way to a majority of families. A critic of what was at one time faddishly called the Adult Child Movement, sarcastically exclaimed, "Why don't you just say that anybody with less than perfect parents becomes an adult child?!" Tongue-in-cheek or not, this is a fairly accurate statement. Almost anyone with less than perfect parents as a child can have unfinished business as an adult. The further from perfect your parents were (in other words, the more non-cherishing moments you had as a child), the more unfinished business you can have as an adult. Recovery is not a matter of defending or blaming your parents (although this may be a stage some need to work through), but is, rather, a matter of taking responsibility for getting on with your life. "Getting on with your life" may necessitate noting what is lacking in your toolbox of life skills due to those historical deprivations, and then doing some compensatory work–work well worth the effort if one believes that daily vitality is a desirable goal.

It is perhaps best to think of *functionality* on a scale from Low to High. The notion that all families can be divided into just the two categories of "functional" and "dysfunctional" is dualistic, and therefore overly simplistic and misleading. Most families have moments of high functionality, as well as moments of low functionality. The higher the proportion of low functioning moments (episodes of abuse & neglect) to high functioning moments (episodes of affirmation & nurturance) during child-raising years, the more unfinished business there will be for the individual in his/her adulthood.

Another factor that must be considered is the *level of traumatization* created within the individual. This is a mysterious and extremely individualistic factor. Some people walk away from trauma unscathed. Some people walk away apparently unscathed, only to discover later that they had unconsciously repressed or consciously suppressed the effects of the trauma. When the effects of trauma are buried they often surface later in life. We call this usually unwelcome surfacing *activation.* Sometimes the activation is obviously related to historical abuse and neglect, but more often it exhibits itself in a non-straightforward manner, as described in the eight characteristics of the Dysfunctional Family Survivor Syndrome and in the three chapters on implications for relationships, education and business.

Of course, some people don't walk away from trauma at all, and it is quite apparent that they have been damaged, perhaps in many ways, by what has happened to them. Psychiatric hospitals, doctor's offices, and prisons are full of these victims exhibiting unfinished business each in their own way. As the Berlin Wall was a constant reminder of just how terrible Communism could be, so are the painful statistics of our institutions a constant monument to the cruelty against children. The righteousness exhibited by the abusers, neglectors and their enablers will never be sufficient to camouflage the glaring statistics of our health and penal institutions which are filled with survivors of abuse and neglect. The silenced voices of those who did not survive are perhaps the loudest testimony of all.

CHAPTER TWO

LIFE'S TOOLBOX OF SKILLS AND TECHNIQUES

Within the acorn is everything needed to grow the mighty oak tree, except external nourishment and some protection from the elements until it is strong enough to withstand hardships on its own. If the seedling isn't nurtured by its environment it dies or is "stunted." This means that the tree may live, but it will have to endure the results of the deprivations suffered as a seedling. This developmental plan is much the same for humans as well, no matter what the culture, ethnicity or gender of the child.

At conception we possess intrinsically all the things we need to achieve our full potential as wonderfully enlightened and spiritual beings. Our environmental requirement for these abilities to materialize is to be fully cherished. The supervisors of our environment, as determined by natural law, are called "parents." The ideal situation (which almost never happens) requires two very healthy parents to be fully developed as adults, spending most of their time raising the child until it can take care of itself–about two decades in our world today. This implies that the two parents themselves each had two such parents, and they each had two such parents. Unfortunately, the intergenerational legacies of abusive/neglectful child-raising, busy and/or preoccupied lifestyles, and parents' own unfinished business, rarely permit such a phenomenon to occur.

Utilizing the analogy of a toolbox, the child is born with all the tools necessary to achieve its rightful place in the world. Most of the tools are "invisible" at the time of birth. Some will acquire visibility naturally through healthy development, while others must be led out by caregivers. Some of the tools deal with emotions, some with communications, others with interpersonal relationships skills, physical skills, problem-solving and decision-making skills, etc., etc...the list is very long.

For example, suppose the primary caregiver doesn't know how to handle anger in a productive and healthy fashion. Children learn by example, and if the male child watches Father handle anger by pretending it isn't there until one day he explodes over some seemingly trivial matter, how then would the child know differently except to handle his frustrations in this same "manly" fashion? It really isn't much different from parents not knowing how to use a hammer. For some reason (perhaps there is a belief that 'hammers are evil' in this particular family tree) the children are taught to use a pair of pliers (a 'pliers are good' legacy) to drive a nail. Pliers will get the job done, but won't be as effective, or might hurt your fingers or the object being nailed into, but it does "get you by." Sadly enough this is exactly what many people do, "Get by" and believe that's all they deserve, and maybe even feel lucky at that! But "getting by" is hardly why we exist. We know humankind has the potential to rise above the mere mastery of bodily needs and, indeed, choose to develop spiritually.

Just how does the Dysfunctional Family Survivor Syndrome prevent us from making increasingly progressive spiritual choices?

An Explanation

When a dry sponge is squeezed under water, the first molecules of water absorbed go the deepest. When it is squeezed again those same first-in molecules will be the last to exit. Quite simply, this is why parents are so powerful: *They are there first*. Their messages have more power in our lives because of a simple law of human physics: "Two things cannot occupy the same space at the same time." The first message in(grained) concerning a certain topic has the most weight, healthy or not, productive or not. The message goes in and there it stays with great resistance (inertia) to change, healthy or not, productive or not. This is because the human mind has one big operating need besides survival, *The need to be right*! It needs to be right about its conclusions, healthy or not, productive or not.

The need to be right is understandably necessary to function and survive. Upon deciding to cross the street you say to yourself, "It's okay to cross, right?" Without a responding "Right!" from within, you might remain indecisively standing on the corner forever (and someone would have to bring you a pizza every day or so to keep you from starving!). It is important to feel "right" about one's perceptions and decisions in order to move ahead with conviction in one's life. But, not unlike many life issues with dysfunctional family survivors, this need can become confused, and often inappropriately applied.

Because of ineffective child-raising, our ego gets warped with this need to be right even to the point of self-destructive stubbornness, and, indeed, many of us humans might be said to stubbornly die prematurely of "terminal righteousness." Usually, we just get along by justifying our perceptions of the world. We rationalize our shortage of tools and skills in a manner which allows us to be righteous not only about our discomfort, but also about our unfulfilled destiny as fully potentialized human beings. We grow up honestly believing that life is hard, nice people finish last, and true happiness is probably (hopefully) achieved only after death. We even proclaim with t-shirts and bumper stickers such beliefs as "*Life sucks, and then you die*." These attitudes are perpetuated by the Dysfunctional Family Survivor Syndrome in individuals. Also perpetuated are violence, mental illness, criminality, war, terrorism, continuances of child abuse and neglect, and much physical suffering and illness.

The only way to stop the ignorance and violence against self and others in our families, schools, businesses, and society is to:

1) Understand exactly what constitutes abuse and neglect;
2) Refuse to perform or enable further harm;
3) Be able to accurately assess the appearance of the Dysfunctional Family Survivor (DFS) Syndrome symptoms; and,
4) Institute programs that counteract not just symptoms but the underlying causative and perpetuating factors.

"Dealing with symptoms is like locking the armory after the weapons are already in the streets." ...Joseph Califano

CHAPTER THREE

ABUSE & NEGLECT and SUSCEPTIBILITY

The core issues are **abuse, neglect,** and **human susceptibility**. *Abuse* is causing harm (the opposite of protection in the oak tree example) and *neglect* is lack of nurturing (nourishment in the oak tree example). Humans are particularly *susceptible* to long-term effects from abuse and neglect because they are a) very sensitive; b) extremely intelligent; and, c) highly adaptable.

Human Sensitivity

The component that makes people spiritual, empathic, caring, and capable of being supportive and compassionate has a downside; it also makes them hyper-vulnerable to the psychological aftereffects of abuse and neglect. It goes with the territory in that if one is going to care about others, one is also going to be open to potential injury. Compassion is a two way street. As an example, in stress psychology studies the major stressors for an individual are created by loved ones and/or relatives. These are the same people who can also fill a life with meaning, excitement and love.

Worst case scenarios of people driven mad by abuse and neglect because of their sensitivity are those who *internalize* their world of activity, such as catatonics, and those who *externalize* their world of activity, such as sociopathic personality types. Both internalizers and externalizers are reacting against their previous suffering, but in ways that destroy their ability to function in the "normal" world. When they are seen in this context, one realizes one is watching victims in the process of *reenactment*, or doing unto self or others what was done unto them.

Human Intelligence

Humans are quick on the uptake. They usually don't have to be bitten more than once to get the message. Along with this quickmindedness is the ability to not only remember events forever, either consciously or subconsciously, but also to let those stored memories accumulate and affect future behavior. We call this ability *learning*. A little known fact is that children are learning proportionately more the younger they are. In other words, a one day old child is learning more per waking hour than a 5 year old, who is learning more per waking hour than a 15 year old, who is learning more per waking hour than a 25 year old, etc. Again, one of the very things that makes humans so special has a downside. The swinging door of human intelligence has *Tremendous Potential* written on one side and *Damaged Easily* on the other side.

Worst case scenarios of people driven mad by abuse and neglect because of their intelligence are those who *internalize* with hallucinations and creative delusions, and those who *externalize* with conniving, manipulating, or rapist mentalities.

"One form of insanity is making the same mistake over and over and expecting different results." ...Unknown

Human Adaptability

Due in part to our intelligence, humans are incredibly adaptive. We are able to adjust almost instantly to situations in order to get our needs met. This is especially true if we perceive a situation as one that may endanger our survival. This is exactly how abuse and neglect are perceived by the child, i.e., as life-threatening. Those in caregiver positions are the keepers of food, shelter and, most of all, the affection that humans desperately need in order to develop appropriately and healthfully. Abuse and neglect are threats to the supply lines, and children know which side their bread is buttered on, especially when they are infants.

The sacrifice of the child's integrity with self occurs often and quickly, and at the time seems a small price to pay to keep the supply lines open. In the long run, however, it can become another form of living death known as *co-dependence*. Co-dependence is the externalized manifestation of someone driven mad because of their <u>adaptability</u>. The internalized form of adaptability gone haywire is chronic anger and/or anxiety due to a constant fear of losing control.

Addiction as Adaptation

Addiction is the inability to say "No" to an event, substance, or person that causes life-damaging consequences physically, mentally, emotionally, spiritually, socially, or financially. Addiction is a prominent *adaptation* that people manifest internally and act out externally in order to deal with the tear in their soul created by being raised in a dysfunctional environment. At one point in time it seemed the biggest dysfunctional family survivor-manifested disease was alcoholism. Later it was realized that all chemical dependencies were crutches in dealing with *dis-ease* and that alcohol was just one form of drug addiction. Then the disease of co-dependence became apparent and it was realized that chemical addictions were just ways of dealing with the pain of living with the disease of co-dependence. In light of current knowledge, a deeper revelation is possible. This book proposes that the major addiction in this world is the addiction to abuse itself. Alcoholism, drug addiction, co-dependence, etc., are just vehicles for abusing the self and others.

Hypothesis: *Anyone with a less than nurturing family of origin easily develops a process addiction to some form of abuse.*

This process addiction is a direct result of abuse/neglect in any form by primary caregivers which resulted in damage to the child's pristine self-esteem. This means that the child learned to disregard the true self and began to adapt by adopting a false self in order to be more pleasing to caregivers. This self-defeating adaptation is perpetuated through an inner drive to affirm subjective conclusions about reality through internal and external reenactments. The denigrating message that is learned and repeated to the self over and over is, "I am the kind of person who needs and/or deserves abuse and/or neglect." And then, in order to be correct about this belief, the survivor attracts and creates a self-fulfilling flight plan of abuse and neglect. Judging by the list in Appendix I, there is no shortage of ways in which this prophecy can be fulfilled.

Without intervention, the means to abuse self and others physically, emotionally, mentally, or sexually are continually discovered by dysfunctional family survivors. There is also an attraction to affiliating with other "carriers" who become part of the drama. And it is a drama. This is not the Plan, no matter how frequently it occurs and how normal it appears. We only need to remember Naziism to know that just because millions of people declare certain actions sane doesn't make them so.

The "True Plan" becomes evident just by watching a human baby born into a secure environment with a low-trauma delivery system. The baby is genuine: WYSIWYG (What You See Is What You Get). It is fully real and pure as an Angel. It even smells sweet. Its emotional expressions are exactly proportional to its own interpretation of reality, not someone else's that it has become co-dependent upon. Because of the power of its purity it will activate anyone around it! We are tantalized by the newborn's ability to reflect, not unlike a mirror, our own unfinished family of origin business. If we were abused as an infant we may feel a need to hurt the child and/or modify its behavior so it won't be so genuine, i.e., make it smile when it doesn't want to, make it stop crying because it bothers us, make it sleep when it apparently wants to be awake, make it eat when it isn't hungry, etc. ad infinitum. The infant has the need to survive like the rest of us, and adapts to the tune of reinforcement, real or perceived. Thus it begins to abandon its Self and the pattern of abuse is formed. And, since we all do it, it appears quite normal. But, of course, adult survivors don't really know what normal is–one of the major characteristics of the Dysfunctional Family Survivor Syndrome.

The baseline premise behind all received abuse is that, "I am not acceptable as I am." If I am being *abused* (a self-validated subjective experience) then I know I am not being cherished at this moment for what and who I am, and I feel *mistrustful* and *ashamed*. If this becomes a recurring pattern in my childhood, I develop a *core of mistrust and shame*. This core, not unlike plutonium rods (energizing but insulated and hidden) in nuclear reactors, becomes a toxic driving force, motivating destructive behavior inwardly (self-abuse) and/or outwardly (other-abuse). Because of its widespread nature it can, indeed, become second nature. It infiltrates our families, our schools, our industry and our institutions. It is highly contagious, enabling it to spread rapidly from person to person and generation to generation. A personality core of mistrust and shame is the fundamental cause of the Dysfunctional Family Survivor (DFS) Syndrome.

So the one fish swims up to the other fish and says,
"What do you think of this water today?"
And the other fish replies, "What water?"

Would we feel like fish out of water without abuse and neglect in our daily lives? If so, do we not then invest in keeping it around and inside us?

CHAPTER FOUR

THE MANY FORMS OF ABUSE

Breaking the addictive cycle of abuse begins with awareness. Awareness is not always comfortable. Awareness of abuse is never comfortable. It is, however, necessary to become aware in order to break the vicious cycle. To paraphrase William Blake:

> *"In order to escape from prison, the first thing you must do is realize that you are in one."*

Towards a Nomenclature of Human Abuse & Neglect

In Appendix I, I have developed a numbering system of the varied forms of abuse and neglect aimed at universal adoption. I encourage everyone to use it, discuss it, and forward their input for modification until it crystallizes into its final form. There are several powerful rationale behind this attempt to classify. A main reason is it appears to be the only method which can provide a language that will communicate to people with legislative power in a way they can both relate and refer to with confidence.

The task is to develop a clarifying nomenclature, or definitive classification system, of abuse and neglect in order to help encourage an accurate universal language for utilization by the public and professional sectors alike. This system will greatly clarify communications regarding traumatic incidents in people's lives. The goals accomplished by adopting a nomenclature would be:

1) Recognition of exact practices that are universally abusive/neglectful

2) Clear definition of abuse/neglect forms

3) Establishment of a coded classification system for clear and concise denotation and documentation

4) Provision of a foundation for the establishment of an accurate database for assessing the short- and long-term effects, including cost factors, of abuse/neglect on human beings

5) Precipitation of a set of standards upon which to evaluate the current projected effectiveness of specific behaviors and practices utilized with children

6) Provision of an accurate assessment system by which society's health, education, legal, and human welfare agencies can make critical decisions affecting defenseless children and their futures

*****

With the standards set by the Classification System of Child Abuse and Neglect (CSCAN) in Appendix I, all of us have probably abused others, have allowed others to abuse us, and/or have abused ourselves. We are probably going to continue to do these things. The question is: Do we wish the abuse to increase, stay the same, or decrease in frequency? If we wish it to decrease, we must become more aware of all of the forms of abuse, including the subtle ones which we erroneously pass off as "harmless." While reading the list in Appendix I, it helps to breathe circularly with a relaxed exhale. Again, just for yourself, please note where this seems difficult.

Definition of Abuse & Neglect

In Appendix I, *abuse* is viewed as an act of commission, and *neglect* is an act of omission. Despite the context commonly assumed and usually reinforced by the media that inflicting physical harm has more impact than any other form, what is true is that the long-term psychological effects of both abuse and neglect are similar. Abuse is obviously overtly harmful, while neglect is, although covert, still abusive. It might even be stated that neglect often creates *more* harmful effects because it is more difficult to identify and, therefore, is not seen for the toxic agent that it is.

***Abuse*: An act which is not accidental and harms, or threatens to harm, a person's physical, mental, or emotional health or safety.**

***Neglect*: An act of omission which results, or could result, in the deprivation of essential services necessary to maintain the minimum mental, emotional or physical health of a person.**

Spiritual Abuse: Although not listed as a specific category, all abuse/neglect, no matter what form, is ultimately spiritual abuse because it facilitates the creating of a **false survivor-self**. This is essentially a separation from the genuine Self, the epitome of spiritual abuse. One of the greatest tragedies of abuse and neglect is that survivors wander through life never knowing who they really are. Without intervention they cannot find their way home to a restored sense of true Self.

[It is suggested that the reader now turn to Appendix I to review the Classification System of Child Abuse & Neglect (CSCAN) before proceeding further.]

CHAPTER FIVE

THE DYSFUNCTIONAL FAMILY SURVIVOR (DFS) SYNDROME

The Dysfunctional Family Survivor Syndrome is a condition which occurs as a direct result of being raised by anyone other than nurturing caregivers. Many of the following eight personality traits develop in children in order to survive abusive and/or life-threatening environments. Dysfunctional Family Survivors carry these adaptational traits through their growing years and often unnecessarily into adult lives that are then limited by these same strategies. More often these traits in adulthood are legitimized in various ways rather than being seen as pieces of handicapping unfinished business. Having thus been rationalized, they go unaddressed and are easily perpetuated across and down through many family layers. In other words, this life-strangling insidiousness can become an accepted part of a family's legacy to its children for many generations.

1) **CONTROL CONSCIOUSNESS**

Growing up in unstable and unpredictable environments creates chaotic inner feelings and uncertainty. One learns to be watchful and cautious in order to survive. One learns to control emotions, thoughts and behaviors through suppression and denial, hoping that this will help control the self, others and the world. One feels he/she must have some control in order to have predictability in an unpredictable world.

2) **AVOIDING EMOTIONS**

The dysfunctional training received as children instilled a denial of what was felt: "Don't trust any of your emotions to benefit you and ignore what your senses tell you." When adults showed emotion it was often associated with abusive situations and children assume a direct cause and effect relationship. The message is, "Don't trust others and their emotions, and don't trust your own emotions either."

3) **INABILITY TO GRIEVE**

Especially noteworthy in dysfunctional family survivors is the inability to grieve losses to completion. The "tunnel of grief" has four sequential stations: 1) shock & denial; 2) anger and/or fear/bargaining; 3) sadness; and, 4) acceptance and/or gratitude. Inability to grieve means that with each need-to-let-go situation one gets "stuck" in one of the stations and never reaches the stage of acceptance. Changes are constant in life. With each change usually comes a "death," whether it be leaving the first grade for the second, quitting cigarettes, letting go of one's youth, quitting a relationship, or leaving home. Inability to grieve to completion means that there are many survivors in perpetual states of shock, denial, anger, fear, and/or sadness.

4) **GUILT FROM OVERRESPONSIBILITY**

The guilt carried in the dysfunctional family survivor (DFS) core stems from feeling overly responsible for caretakers' actions and feelings. The survivor may even feel guilty for the abuse suffered, and perhaps for any punishment that siblings received. Dysfunctional family survivors often continue into adulthood with a habitual pattern of feeling the need to caretake others.

5) **CRISIS ADDICTION**

Inconsistencies, surprises, and terror perhaps were the norm in the childhood of a DFS, so when things are calm and stable survivors may feel deadened or "bored," thereby necessitating an urge to stir up things. Although they may complain outwardly about chaos, survivors may be uncomfortable deep inside when it is not present. Some DFS develop an excitement addiction, and will generate an "uproar game" if things are too serene. Often this appears as sabotage in school, business or relationships. "They just can't stand success," might be a phrase that sometimes applies to DFSs.

6) **GUESSING AT NORMALITY**

What is normal? Since most dysfunctional family survivors' home lives were extremist in nature, no standards were established for the concept of normality. As they grow, DFSs are constantly confused as to what is really healthy and normal, so they frequently feel unsure inside (although they may have complex strategies to portray themselves as otherwise).

7) **LOW SELF-ESTEEM**

Being abused and neglected delivers the message, "You are not good enough the way you are." When self-adjusting brings the same response again, one perceives "The truth is that no matter what I do, I am not good enough." Thus the core of shame overshadows the pristine self and dysfunctional family survivors regard themselves as defective or irretrievably damaged. It is impossible to develop a benevolent self-concept in this soil. They find many ways to reaffirm the belief that they are, indeed, always "less than" in thoughts, words, and actions. It is this self-validating internalized assumption that delivers the crucifying mandates by which DFSs often shape their lives.

8) **COMPULSIVE BEHAVIORS**

One of the earliest evaluative scales we all learned as infants was pain vs. pleasure. Human beings avoid pain and seek pleasure. The psychological pain of being alienated from the true self is one of the most intense, confusing and enduring possible. It resembles an incurable migraine of the soul. Compulsive behavior of any sort offers an irresistible temptation–anesthesia for the psychological pain and a pleasant diversion for the body. One can be compulsive about almost anything: alcohol and other drugs; work; gambling; food; shopping; hoarding; sex; exercise; relationships; particular emotion lookalikes (rageaholism, sadaholism, phobias); power; money; violence; etc., ad infinitum.

The DFS Syndrome and Limits & Boundaries

If one could locate an underlying theme of the eight characteristics of the DFS Syndrome it would be about distorted external and internal limits and boundaries. *Limits* are self-determined definings of how far I am going to let myself go, i.e., "I am only going to eat 2000 calories today," "I am going to take off at noon today," "I am not going to loan you any more money," etc. *Boundaries* are self-determinations about how far I am going to let 'you' go, e.g., "You cannot talk to me like that," "Don't come over to my house without calling first," "If you hit me I will call the police," "Don't ask me that anymore," etc.

The simplest definition for a "good upbringing" that I can come up with is one in which a child learns how to healthfully set limits and boundaries for themselves in such a way that they prosper physically, mentally, emotionally, socially and spiritually for the rest of their lives. Dysfunctional upbringing wreaks havoc with this very ability. Look back over the eight DFS Syndrome characteristics and interpret them with *limits & boundaries* in mind.

Recovery

Recovery is the process of working to uncover the natural self that there might be restoration to a balanced way of life. In this way the DFS can enjoy being true to his/her and other's genuine selves. Recovery is often accomplished through 12-

step groups, counseling, and support groups, which are all various means of personally resetting limits & boundaries. Sometimes more concentrated recovery work is necessary, such as treatment, rehabilitation, and/or medication, which are all means of having structured limits & boundaries established for the individual. A general rule of thumb is that the more intense the abuse and neglect was, the more intense the recovery work will usually have to be.

[A special acknowledgement goes to Steven Farmer for his pioneering work in the recovery field, and for his assistance in developing the Dysfunctional Family Survivor characteristic list. Steven is Director of Steven Douglas Farmer & Associates in Laguna Beach, California, and is author of four books, among them *The Wounded Male* and *Adult Children of Abusive Parents*.]

NOTE: The next three chapters look at the implications of the Dysfunctional Family Survivor Syndrome for three of our most popular institutions: human relationships; education; and, the work place. The chapters are not meant to be all inclusive —each chapter could be turned into a volume, if not a set of volumes. The purpose of the next three chapters is to quickly give the reader a flavor of a) how this thing called the DFS Syndrome looks in action, and/or b) some insights that might show strategic intervention possibilities. There are even a few very direct suggestions.

CHAPTER SIX

Implications of the
Dysfunctional Family Survivor Syndrome
RELATIONSHIPS'

[This chapter was written especially for this book
by Steven Farmer, author
Adult Children as Husbands, Wives, & Lovers]

1) CONTROL CONSCIOUSNESS

Strategies for controlling your mate

The following are some of the more common ways survivors use to manipulate their partners into reacting certain ways, such as feeling guilty or intimidated, or to avoid certain reactions from their partner, such as anger or disapproval. These are largely unconscious re-enactments of the survival patterns learned while growing up in the dysfunctional family, and while their original purpose was survival, in adulthood they usually no longer serve that purpose. Instead they are conditioned habit patterns that maintain an illusion of safety in that they are familiar and the outcome is predictable. When they become routine behaviors in relationship, however, they end up with both partners feeling a deeper dissatisfaction, alienation, and lack of love and intimacy.

Withholding - Silence can be one of the most powerful controlling behaviors a survivor can have in his/her repertoire, especially if the partner reacts by feeling guilty. In the early stages of the relationship, withholding may not have been a control strategy, but merely an inability to express certain feelings, such as anger or sadness. As the relationship progresses, however, silent, fuming anger can become the weapon of choice in conflict. The partner using this strategy can become inaccessible. With a few years of practice, this can deaden both the individual and the relationship. A classic example of this is when one partner says to the other, "What's bothering you?" and the mate replies, "Nothing!" with an abrupt, sharp tone of voice, hands folded across the chest, and a scowl on the face.

Martyrdom - The martyr is always doing for others, not simply out of kindness, but from a foundation of self-sacrifice learned in the family of origin. When it becomes controlling and manipulative in adult relationships, the objective is to get others to suffer as well - with guilt. The martyr often "suffers in silence," communicating this by mournful sighs and a bedraggled expression. The aim of this is to communicate, "Look how much of a burden I'm carrying! Can't you see how put upon I am!" Yet most offers of help by the partner (which would end the game) get rejected .

Helplessness - This strategy is used to stay safe, and is expressed by passivity, confusion and uncertainty. While everyone feels these at times, the survivor's unconscious objective in staying in this condition is to stay safe, to never be a threat to the partner. Another term for this could be "helpless victim." The one who takes on this role is constantly looking for a "rescuer." The only problem is that the rescuer will inevitably fail, and in the eyes of the helpless victim, that person then becomes a perpetrator. [See TRIANGULATION in Appendix III.]

Lying - The aim of lying is usually to look good, or at least avoid looking bad in order to maintain an image of "good boy/girl." In adulthood, if the lying continues, it can range from mild "little white lies" to major lies, such as infidelity. He/she experiences this as a split, sort of a "good self/bad self," and tries to present the "good self" front to his partner while hiding the "bad self" in shame and secrecy. When this becomes an habitual strategy of control, the person ends up living a duplicitous life, eventually driving a wedge between the two partners.

Bullying - This is the most overt strategy of control in that the partner using this is physically and or verbally aggressive in a direct attempt to intimidate, coerce or overpower the mate. It is an abuse of power learned from the models in childhood. Beneath the exterior of bullying lies a very insecure individual, deathly afraid that the partner will abandon ship. Obviously one danger in this is that it can lead to violence, but even more insidious is the toxicity that builds up over time for the one who is the object of this bullying, as well as for the relationship.

2) AVOIDING EMOTIONS

The implications for an adult survivor's relationship in this area are profound. When you are trained to avoid emotions, or can only express one emotion, e.g. anger, intimacy becomes extremely difficult, if not impossible. There are two elements to consider in understanding how a survivor continues to avoid emotions in adult relationships: Family Rules and Post-Traumatic Stress Disorder (PTSD).

Family Rules - DON'T TALK; DON'T TRUST; DON'T FEEL. These rules were first identified by Claudia Black as originating inside the dysfunctional family. They remain consistent for most survivors into adulthood. Don't Talk - You get scolded, shamed, abused or ignored for telling your truth. Family secrets might be exposed if you speak up. Don't Trust - Since inconsistency and unpredictability were the norm, there was little you could rely on. Plus, your perceptions were denied. In adulthood you learn to distrust your own sensory cues, thereby still mistrusting what you perceive. Don't Feel - Feelings, both awareness of them and their expression, were denied, ignored or threatened with punishment. So it's no surprise that this would be carried into adulthood.

If these three rules remain operative in adulthood, then feeling anything at all, let alone trusting and expressing those feelings, is simply not done. If one or both partners is operating with these rules, then communication inevitably shuts down.

PTSD - Psychic numbing is one of the symptoms of Post-Traumatic Stress Disorder, a psychiatric diagnosis originally designated for survivors of war. The symptoms parallel those of adult survivors, and the one symptom that has the most to do with avoiding emotions is psychic numbing.

More than avoidance, the human being's animal body simply shuts down under situations of extreme stress, especially if the stress lasts for years. We become less capable of experiencing physical sensations, which provide the sensory cues for our emotional feelings. Since emotional and sensory exchanges are an important part of any relationship, having these dulled by psychic numbing will interfere with developing intimacy in a relationship.

3) INABILITY TO GRIEVE

Since survivors tend to have their emotional experience dulled, it follows that they have difficulty with the important and necessary grief work that is so much a part of being human. Shutting down our ability to grieve tends to shut down the upper range of feelings (joy, happiness) as well. If we don't grieve the normal losses that are a part of life, we remain inaccessible to our partner. As Carl Jung said, "Every neurosis is a lack of legitimate suffering." The less we share of our legitimate suffering or grief with our partner, the harder it becomes to share the joys. This further reinforces the pattern of shutting down and avoiding, resulting in greater emotional and spiritual distance.

4) GUILT FROM OVERRESPONSIBILTY

The childhood training in a dysfunctional family falsely teaches a child that they are the cause of many of the upsets and miseries in the family. This is carried over into adult relationships by a partner who often feels anxious and guilty much of the time because he/she automatically concludes that when something goes wrong, or the partner is upset or unhappy, it's somehow his/her fault, whether or not the partner is actually doing active blaming. Like the Paul Simon song, "When something goes wrong I'm the first to admit it but the last one to know."

The partner who uses this strategy often experiences a continual, low-level anxiety and general passivity, and does things to placate the partner in an attempt to magically ward off any blame or conflict. Another version is extreme defensiveness, with a constant need to explain and justify. One partner says to the other, "Did you get the tickets for the concert yet?" in a non-accusatory way, and the other launches into a lengthy explanation of why he/she hasn't.

5) CRISIS ADDICTION

Having adapted to the chaos and unpredictability that are the norm in a dysfunctional family, the child becomes accustomed to the rush of adrenalin that comes with continual forays into survival mode. The child's vigilance can never totally relax, because he never knows when the next uproar will take place. Having become familiar with this way of operating, the survivor will unconsciously seek out or else create crisis/trauma/drama in his/her lives simply because it is so familiar. One becomes an "adrenalin junkie" and needs a fix regularly, so when things are calm and steady and going well, it may feel like fingernails on a chalkboard. When everything is calm for too long a partner will find some reason to stir things up, resulting in the unpleasant but familiar chaos and conflict that reigned true in the family of origin.

6) GUESSING AT NORMALITY

Since characteristics of dysfunctional families are typically ones of extremes, it's difficult for a child growing up in this atmosphere to have a sense of normality. As an adult in relationship, knowing what normal feelings and behaviors are is a mystery. The survivor often doubts and second guesses: "Is this okay to do? Is it normal to feel this? Should I be acting this way?" The partner will likely idealize the self and the relationship, trying to fit that ideal, yet finding that she/he and the partner will inevitably fall short.

Many survivors do not know that conflict is a part of any relationship, that it can lead to resolution, and that abusiveness does not have to be part of that conflict. Many survivors don't know that distance and closeness wax and wane, that love does not mean obsessive attachment, that any relationship over time will go through developmental adjustments, that jealousy, anger, sadness, and tenderness are legitimate aspects of any relationship.

Typically the survivor must do some research on this one, by talking with trusted friends and advisors, getting counseling, and selecting from the abundance of books and articles on the subject of adult survivors.

7) LOW SELF ESTEEM

One of the psychic wounds left from the ongoing abusive or neglectful environment in a dysfunctional family is low self-esteem. The adult survivor with low self-esteem in relationship may manifest this by being negative and self-critical, perhaps even frequently depressed. He/she looks to his partner for continual validation, yet never truly believes the response. Another way is to project his/her sense of inadequacy onto the partner and continually berate and criticize him/her in order to provide a temporary yet false sense of power and self-worth.

Another way is to mask this low self-esteem with anger and bullying or with compulsive-addictive behaviors. These are all ways to escape or avoid the unpleasant feelings that typically accompany low self-esteem. Any way this manifests, the survivor with low self-esteem is often unhappy and brings the weight of this unhappiness to the partner.

8) COMPULSIVE BEHAVIORS

When acting out compulsive-addictive behaviors, the individual drives a wedge between himself/herself and the partner. This happens because the inevitable consequences of compulsive behaviors are denial, secretiveness, promises not kept, emotional distance, and a downward spiral of personal and relationship deterioration. With compulsive-addictive behavior, much time is dedicated toward the acting out of the particular compulsive behavior, so that this becomes the priority above most everything else.

The one with the most obvious compulsive-addictive behavior will often attract someone who is co-dependent. For instance, the alcoholic will attract someone who will participate in the alcoholic game of denial, inadvertently supporting the alcoholic's addiction and spiral of deterioration. Whatever the compulsive-addictive behavior, often the survivor's mate will participate by avoidance and/or denial that the compulsive-addictive behavior is a problem. Eventually these compulsive-addictive behaviors will drive a couple apart, especially if the couple is doing the dance of denial.

CHAPTER SEVEN

Implications of the Dysfunctional Family Survivor Syndrome in the EDUCATIONAL ENVIRONMENT

Children bring unfinished business to school in their pencil and lunch boxes and educators bring their unfinished business in brief cases. At the starting bell they snap open their respective containers and throw the contents on each other all day. It wears everyone out and is usually given the general title of "discipline problem." Due to misidentification and ignorance nothing ever gets resolved, can even be made worse, and everyone usually winds up frustrated, resentful, and depressed. Usually the only "creative" response is that the school policy manuals get thicker every year. The first DFS Syndrome symptom - control consciousness - is ironically never more appropriate than in the educational environment.

1) CONTROL CONSCIOUSNESS

Schools are mostly about *control.* Can the kids control their urges and learn to delay gratification? Can the teachers control themselves enough so that they will be the kind of educational technicians that can create that magical thing known as the learning environment? Can the administrators control their images, energy levels, budgets, and staff in order not to look bad and yet still carry out the edicts created by the school board/public/parents/business leaders/changing times/ etc.?

A trained family systems therapist can walk through a school and after listening to a few minutes of several conversations and watching the corresponding body language, interpret for you a whole universe of the unfinished family business that really resides behind most interactions in the school. It's all about fear - the fear of losing control. Although the therapist's interpretation will be correct, nobody will want to hear it, will deride and promptly ignore it. This is because the interpretation is right on the money. And it hurts.

Every year our schools are becoming bigger and bigger catch basins of unfinished family of origin business influencing every person in them. I wouldn't teach in a school of today unless the staff was aware of this. Dysfunction is most dangerous when denied, meaning that more dysfunctionality is being perpetrated even as denial is occurring. This is what we mean by a "highly toxic environment." In their ignorance and denial some professionals are treating poison victims with just bigger doses of poison. And it's all done in a futile effort to heal the pain, or at least control it.

Control modalities for children

It is natural for healthy children to want to learn, grow and develop. We assume the school environment and its personnel are encouraging this development. But what if the child is blocked from natural progress due to its own dysfunctional control mechanisms learned from a dysfunctional home? How might we identify those modalities?

Retreat modalities- Passivity, shyness, withdrawn, phobic, anxious, fearful, and spiritual limpness, are various expressions of someone suffering from a general mistrust that the "facts are friendly." For that person, life perhaps has become a series of abusive/neglectful episodes, and the best strategy is to run as far away as possible. It makes sense. It looks odd when the reaction is there although the threat isn't apparent in the school environment, but we must remember that we carry our historical universe with us in our internal microclimate and <u>that</u> is where we react from. Think of these individuals as having retreated into the recesses of a cave as far as they can go. It's lonely and damp in there, but it appears safer than what masquerades as life-giving sunlight outside the cave. In what way could you reassure these cave dwellers that they could dare take the risk to come out and try once more to develop? Once you get them out, what would you have to do to sustain that trust? (Also see "Tunnel of Grief " below.)

Aggressive modalities- A good offense is the best defense. Sound familiar? This is a fairly accurate truism in our world today. Its roots are in childhood. Let's be honest, we admire someone who fights back, who stands up on their hind legs after being abused and growls, "Enough!" Why don't we admire this spunk in kids? Because it's often misplaced. They can't fight their abusers and neglectors. Either they don't know who the abusers are because it was camouflaged or justified, or it's too dangerous to confront the offender. (Did you stand up and growl at your parents when they cracked you one or called you names, or did you take it out on someone else/yourself?) What do these children need? Acknowledgement of their wounds and a chance to heal them, plus training in how to creatively express their pain. They will also desperately need to learn from a healthy model about how to go about setting limits and boundaries for themselves in society. Schools have an excellent opportunity to be this model. Democracy must be reinvented every generation. The general environmental rule in school should be, "We will give you educational opportunities to set your own healthy limits and boundaries, but if you can't we will do it for you until you can. Our goal is to help you learn how to healthfully self-monitor and self-adjust your life toward quality outcomes."

Mental illness- Few mental patients come from functional homes. Children with mental illness are trying unsuccessfully to fill a need. Mental illness is a means of controlling either the external or internal environment to reduce threat or pain. It may show up in the forms of obsessive behaviors, dissociation, depression, self-abuse, violence, chemical abuse, and/or anti-social behaviors. If you know that at the root of the behavior is a lost child trying to cope, then you can find them in their darkness a lot easier. Be a friend with a flashlight leading them to either healthier patterns or to someone who can teach them healthier patterns. Know your objects of referral.

Overachieving or underachieving- Trying to be more than you are is self-abusive, and trying to be less than you are is self-abusive. A healthy life is accepting yourself as a developing entity with a potentially great, although unknown, future, and feeling good about that. Kids dramatically over- or under-shooting their academic targets are often trying to prove themselves to be somebody they are not and using the curriculum as a vehicle of self-abuse.

2) AVOIDING EMOTIONS

Well, if children aren't emotions what are they? One comical view of school is to see it as a bunch of little emotional agendas running up against a bunch of totally emotionless curriculum guides, policy manuals and schedules. In actuality that is more of a tragedy than a comedy, because it occurs in schools on a daily basis. Children coming out of dysfunctional environments have a screwed up sense about emotions, what they are, and how to express and resolve them appropriately. What is the school's response to this? Answer: A good day is when children have no emotions and just quietly do their work. What should the school's response be? Answer: "Emotions are normal responses–neither good or bad–to the environment, and they have an onset, sequence, and an end. They are indicators of what we love or fear, and, as such, indicate our values. There are healthy ways to experience and benefit from your emotions." Then provide a curriculum to show them how to handle their emotions effectively.

3) INABILITY TO GRIEVE

I have listened to adult clients showing little emotion as they offer up laundry lists of abuses heaped upon them as children. When finished, I would ask them what they did not get as children that they wished they would have, and then the tears and hurt begin to show. Most every one feels ashamed to admit they felt betrayed, ripped off, or denied what we all needed as children: a healthy, loving, safe and nurturing family that accepts - no, *affirms* - us exactly as we are. The shame (which has some misguided sense of sinful selfishness about it) felt by these adult survivors, is what blocks the grief work necessary to finally lay to rest a childhood full of heartbreak.

Children in school exhibit their unfinished grief work in a number of ways. If one looks at the "tunnel of grief" needed to fully complete any separation it facilitates understanding where children might get stuck.

☹ ➔ ➔ ☻

①	②	③	④
DENIAL	ANGER	SADNESS	GRATITUDE
SHOCK	GUILT	EMPTINESS	ACCEPTANCE
NUMBNESS			

TUNNEL OF GRIEF

We can learn about the tunnel of grief by utilizing our own experiences. Take a moment and clearly remember a past separation with which you are not comfortable. In which stage of grief are you still stuck?

Stage 1. SHOCK/DENIAL/NUMBNESS

Are you still "numb"? Do you say, "I can't bear to think about it."? Do you have difficulty in remembering it? Does it seem faint and far away? Does your mind have trouble focussing on that past separation?

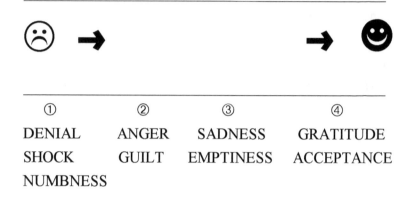

Stage 2. ANGER/GUILT

Are you resentful? Do you feel cheated or ripped-off? Could it be that you really need to feel anger but won't let yourself because it may appear trivial, selfish, silly, or futile? Or do you feel angry at yourself (guilt) for not doing all you feel you should have done?

Stage 3. SADNESS/EMPTINESS

Are you "depressed" about it? Feel the need to cry about it? Inconsolable? Hurt? Empty? Lost? Lonely? Exhausted?

Stage 4. GRATITUDE/ACCEPTANCE

Do you see how you benefitted from the experience, person, or thing from which you are now separated? Do you feel peaceful or pleasant when you remember? Do you have insight as to how that experience/person/thing has helped you to cope better with your life today?

Know that if the separation was highly traumatic you may need to go through the tunnel of the same event more than once in order to peel the internal layers of the tunnel. It is comforting to know that each layer is easier and faster than the previous one. One day, when you have completely "cored out" the tunnel, it will vanish leaving only nostalgia and gratitude.

There are three helpful things to remember while in the middle of the grieving process: 1) It is natural, healthy, and necessary to grieve the many separations we must pass through in our lifetime; 2) It is helpful to *breathe* in nice slow circles with a relaxed exhale when experiencing grief (this allows the body to surrender to the truth of your emotions); and, 3) Know in your heart that this pain is temporary - that it will pass, contrary to the feeling that it seems endless.

The grief process is about becoming honest and taking responsibility for our emotional lives. Successful grief work liberates us from our past, allows us to ride easy in the saddle of the present, and promotes enthusiasm about our ability to handle whatever the future may bring.

So, back to our major point, we may find kids in various stages of grief at any time. Students who are called "airheads" or "daydreamers" or "unconscious" are probably in the first stage of grief and don't know how to get out. They are in shock, denial, or just numb from the experiences of abuse/neglect. "Angry kids" have been denied the love which they need and are feeling ripped off. Sad children are experiencing the void or seemingly endless sea of emptiness. A professional educator moves children through the stages to gratitude and acceptance so they can get to a "Now what?" state of being naturally, and can begin to rebuild their lives in a manner deserved from the beginning.

4) GUILT FROM OVERRESPONSIBILITY

Probably the saddest children to witness are the ones who try to become little adults too soon. Unfortunately, we often mistakenly call these children "good" as they more than likely become overachievers or even "little helpers" for the teachers. It is important to look behind the scenes here and make sure that we are not enabling an already unhealthy pattern. Children are not supposed to be developing such broad shoulders when they have such brittle bones. If this is not discouraged they will grow up into classic enablers themselves.

Guilt is all about breaking rules or standards. The guilt-ridden statement "I am not a good person" means that I have not lived up to the standards of goodness. But just whose standards of goodness have been internalized, and are they clear, healthy and appropriate? Children trying to grow up too fast are often attempting to be surrogate parents or even spouses in the name of "goodness." This easily kills the precious flower of childhood.

5) CRISIS ADDICTION

Kamikaze kids: They look like they can't stand success. Just when things are starting to go well, they "screw it up." If this applies to a child in your life or school environment, then know that this is the symptom being played out. With some children this is the only time they feel electrically alive. With others, although it may look like they "just want attention", it is the strategy they have adopted to get a semblance of affection – negative attention being better than none at all, just like bad breath is better than no breath at all. These children need to be shown more appropriate paths to get their needs met. They need positive attention when things are calm, or means of getting affection without playing the uproar game.

6) GUESSING AT NORMALITY

How could kids coming out of some of the homes they do have even an approximation of what the concept of *normal* means? They have been in a pool of such craziness and abuse/neglect that their standards are either warped or nonexistent. The school must model sanity and a limits and boundaries system based on a range of acceptable normalcy. Again, democracy must be reinvented every generation. Children usually must rely on the school to learn the wonderful system of concern for peers built upon the Three Musketeers slogan, "All for one and one for all!" If the school cannot establish this productive "counterculture" for a child, then all is usually lost for that particular individual. Fair or not, the school is often the last bastion for teaching sane and healthy social interaction. If the school itself is a poor example, then the only safety net for these children is a life of institutions, prisons, or death.

7) LOW SELF-ESTEEM

Children are born with naturally healthy (some call this "high") self-esteem and it becomes covered over with a lot of environmental pollution in a dysfunctional family. The school's function is to provide a counteracting force where children can prove to themselves that they deserve the self-esteem with which they were born. Unfortunately, schools often unwittingly revictimize the victim. This is often done out of just pure ignorance and naivete. Schools, although they should know better by now, still naively expect children to come to school with all their "oars in the water." When the kids don't fit the expectations of the curriculum guides or normed behavioral standards for their grade levels, they are then seen as little cognitive deficits, and are either discarded or, with well-intentioned (but still poisonous) tongue-clucking, patronizingly labeled and treated like moronic cattle – none of which serves to uncover the healthy self-esteem needing to be expressed.

Success is the greatest esteem-builder. If an educational system is so deficiency-based (always looking for what is missing rather than what is present) that it is unaware of constantly sending the all too familiar message to the child: "Oh, and another thing wrong with you is..." then it becomes an enabler of the soul-killing system already established for the child by his/her dysfunctional home environment.

8) COMPULSIVE BEHAVIORS

Here I want to lump addictive and compulsive behaviors together. Let us just agree that we are discussing children who are into destructive cycles of behaviors or habits that they cannot say "No" to. Again, compulsive-addictive behaviors are actually a form of mental illness, but many of them have become an acceptable norm in large parts of our society. We easily become blind to them because as classic dysfunctional members of the bigger societal family ourselves we have developed a high tolerance for inappropriate behavior and pain. But just because we have gotten used to cigarette smoking, alcohol consumption, gambling, hypo- and hyper-eating problems, etc., does not take away their destructive impact on individuals and society.

A healthy school environment, by definition, must establish a confrontive (truth-telling) attitude toward self-destructive behaviors and, if it has the resources, provide support for recovery from such behaviors. Here is where good role-modeling, school support groups, school counselors and psychologists, and satellite services pay off. Compulsive-addictive behavior patterns are tough to break because they give a little shot of pleasure along with a lot of temporary relief from pain (no wonder they are so prevalent!), so the countermeasures have to be commensurately healthy and determined enough for a fight that will last the long haul. Confrontation does work, as statistics have shown in systems that have targeted specific destructive patterns with hard-hitting programs. Always expect a fight. Nobody wants to give up their placebo, because it feels like the only life raft on the ocean to them. The answer is to provide a more attractive raft.

CHAPTER EIGHT

Implications of the Dysfunctional Family Survivor Syndrome in the WORK ENVIRONMENT

Adult survivors grow up with their inappropriate, yet sometimes remarkably workable, social tools and skills learned (or not) in the dysfunctional home environment and sail off into the work place with them. Many times they don't work well and the person is filtered out of the organization sooner (sometimes before they even get in) or later. Some organizations "inherited" workers (or even owner-managers) with problems and have to live with the results. Progressive companies have human resources departments that may or may not recognize dysfunctional family survivors (DFS) and may or may not have effective programs or agencies to handle such issues. My purpose here is to at least spotlight some of the ways in which the DFS Syndrome manifests itself in order to facilitate diagnosis and possible intervention in the work place. It is obviously a touchy and complex area of concern in a complicated and confusing arena. Business and industry would benefit greatly from thorough investigative research into the issues raised in the work environment caused by unfinished family of origin business.

1) CONTROL CONSCIOUSNESS

Business incorporates control or it won't be a business for long. The way of the world is erosion. If one does not mount at least an equal and opposite controlling force against them the erosive forces of time and nature will wear things away as part of the natural order of birth and decay and rebirth. But what kind of control? To what end? By what means and guidelines? Subject to whose authority? These are all legitimate business questions that need to be answered. They often get confused with another form of control, namely an individual's attempt to control his or her personal life and destiny. In the ideal work environment there would be that wonderful symbiosis, where the organization was both aware and willing to help the individual employee fulfill his/her goals and the individual felt the same towards the company's goals. But, as mentioned, these frequently and easily get confusingly blended together.

Employees exhibit control consciousness with some familiar strategies. Some they learned in their families and schools and act out in their intimate relationships too, so it would behoove the reader of this section to read the other two chapters on implications and see how they might interpolate into the work environment. I would like to mention a few specific to the work environment.

Anxiety- Unnecessary fears and worrying are common strategies for attempting to control one's inner and outer world. Taken to an extreme they become phobias or obsessive, and truly become counterproductive. Once ingrained they become a vicious cycle of self-fulfilling prophecy and tension. Some management teams keep people "motivated" with anxiety as the kicker. This is not a healthy company and its employee statistics probably show it.

Abuse- People "hammer" themselves or each other with various forms of mental, emotional and, sometimes even physical abuse (See Appendix II). Why? Answer: To control for different outcomes. Why this chronic pattern exists, when research has proven over and over again that positive achievement-oriented reinforcement works better, can only be explained in two ways: *ignorance* (they just don't know any better yet) or *habit* (a deeply ingrained reflexive pattern of response that is, at best, inappropriate and, at worst, mindlessly destructive. Abuse in the workplace should be treated like a cancer and eliminated. First, it must be diagnosed and labeled (using Appendix II is a good start), next the populace must be educated, then consequences must be established and followed – just as we have with the issues of sexual harassment, child labor laws, gender equity, racial discrimination, etc.

Physical Illness- Physical illness and accidents are often an indicator of attempts at control. It is the body of the individual expressing its own wisdom in the establishing of a safety net. Migraines, sore backs and other body parts, nausea, digestive problems, and cardiac issues are common physiological responses to *stress,* the need or inability to control a change.

Gossip and back-stabbing- These nasty little procedures are incubated and hatched in dysfunctional families. They are seen as "safe" ways to bleed off fear, excitation, and anger. They are a poor substitute for healthy confrontation, but once the energy is dissipated by the unhealthy patterns there is no pressure to confront any longer. This can become an habitual pattern of response to authority figures, and finds natural expression in many work environments. A good rule to implement that will neutralize this whole destructive pattern is that you cannot talk about anyone negatively unless they are standing in front of you. If everyone abided by this what a sweet place the work environment would be!

Workaholism- Let's end the confusion. Working hard is not workaholism. Being unable to stop working hard even when it endangers your health is workaholism. Habitually overworking at a job you resent turns into workaholism. Being driven, preoccupied, and obsessed with work even when quitting time has long come and gone can be a sign of workaholism. Confusing one's *self* and *worth* with one's work is a sign too. Hard work by itself is not a sign. Loving your work and wishing there were more hours in the day to do it is not a sign. Being unable to say "No" <u>is</u> a sign. Workaholism is all about an unhealthy means of controlling image, fears, and others. It is a sickness, and like all illnesses can and will lead to premature death.

Money addiction- Similar to work addiction, but this is more about the end products of work than the processes itself, namely $$$. Money, of course, is a great controller of appearance. It enables one to purchase the things that can fend off insecurity, control one's image, and manipulate others. For some, it becomes like a drug, a lover, and an obsession. There may appear to be a thin line between a healthy awareness of and capability with money, and a downright addiction. The best assessment comes with distance and time. Is the individual becoming more and more "crusty" and preoccupied with money? Is it filling their lives (thoughts, words, and actions) more and more, replacing activities with loved ones, healthy pursuits, recreation, vacations, etc.? The old adage is that "If what you want is not what you need you will never get enough." Never is this saying more true than with money addiction.

2) AVOIDING EMOTIONS

True or False: Emotions have no place in the work environment? This would be a workable truth as long as one could refrain from adding that sticky little factor to the formula: people. People are pretty much emotional beings if nothing else. We must also remember that any experience we have has an emotional component, even if we are not consciously aware of it. So, an emotionless atmosphere in a work place is extremely uncomfortable for someone who is healthy. Certain fields of occupation (which I will not name here) attract people who are able to cap their emotions, and create the appearance of a well-oiled machine, until you get "inside" and you see how the emotions are coming out "sideways" all over the place. The answer is not to deny but to admit emotions as a reasonably anticipated part of all life, especially at work where there are so many deadlines, expectations, and non-preferred activities and relationships.

We should note that emotions do no harm, but resisting emotions has wreaked havoc personally and organizationally! We must get over the absolutely zany idea that strength is synonymous with suppression of emotion. If anything is a weakening factor it is the denial of one's humanity which leaves one vulnerable to a plethora of psychosomatic and social problems.

3) INABILITY TO GRIEVE

The older you get the more losses it seems you must grieve. The work place is not excluded. With every change involving the severance of an attachment, there is at least a little grief work necessary. It could be changing shifts, changing jobs, locations, the personnel one associates with, etc. When people cannot grieve they stuff. They often chronically stuff at the same station in the "tunnel of grief" depending on their personality. Some people are just in a state of numbness or denial (Stage 1). Others are always angry (Stage 2). Some are always sad (Stage 3). Others know how to get through the tunnel and live in a state of acceptance and gratitude most of the time. It takes knowledge of the tunnel and practice with its stations for people to give themselves permission to feel their grief as a normal part of life.

DFS are almost always ignorant about grief and are frequently the ones mentioned previously that are locked into one of the first three stages. Their families frequently were not healthy emotionally which resulted in emotions getting a "bad rap" so they could not be expressed healthfully. Another complicating factor is that there is such a large sum total of losses to be grieved in a dysfunctional family, which results in an incredible backlog of unfinished grief work for each individual coming from that environment.

4) GUILT FROM OVERRESPONSIBILITY

This shows up at work as the "broad shoulders - brittle bones" worker I mentioned in the chapter on educational implications. Those expressing this symptom may become people-pleasing slaves or martyrs or little goody go-getters that perturb other people for some reason when it looks like they are doing everything right. The reason they are perturbing is because they have a hidden agenda or a secret "price tag." Somebody (anybody) is going to pay for them being so "good." You may have to listen to them deliver their litany of accomplishments and sacrifices, or be terribly thankful to them for their incredible performances, all the while feeling like you wish you were somewhere else. Your price tag: Be a phony and feign interest. These people frequently have many illnesses and/or family problems that are part of their crucifix. Sooner or later everything comes crashing in on them. They need help and yet they pretend to be the helpers.

5) CRISIS ADDICTION

There could be no place more suitable for a collection of golden opportunities for the crisis addict than the work place.

It is a veritable breeding ground for tight deadlines, cantankerous computers and machinery, personal differences, supply problems, *ad infinitum*. In other words there are enough natural problems, decisions and stresses that the flames don't need additional fanning. But this is exactly what a crisis addict does. When things are going smoothly they feel agitated, so they create a crisis in order to soothe their feelings. Some psychologists have suggested that this is caused by crisis addicts coming out of such threatening childhood environments that they spent most of their time numbed out to the excitement of life's normal ups and downs. They only broke through the protective numbness and felt truly "alive" during a time of crisis, and since we all want to be alive, being in a crisis becomes a DFS equivalent to "living."

6) GUESSING AT NORMALITY

People who guess at what normality is often wind up as either "fluctuators" or "frozen in place." Fluctuators run from one choice to another wondering, or even asserting, that "This is it!" Emotionally they may be acting out all over the place or, the exact opposite, show total withdrawal. They either drink everything in sight or won't touch a drop, and there seems to be no consistent rationale in their choice. They spend like crazy, then are suddenly talking of austere budgets and clipping coupons to save a few pennies here and there. In other words, the concept of *moderation* may be missing from their lives.

Those "frozen in place" have taken a good guess at normality and just chosen to stay that way no matter what, or they may have modeled themselves after someone else and frozen themselves into that identity. The self seen is not the real person but a paper doll of what that person wants you to see. It is their best guesstimate of what they want to be or what they think they should be. It is a life devoid of flexibility and creativity and, therefore, is continually threatened by the winds of change and suddenly being seen as unacceptable or out of step. Intense energy is spent in maintaining the front outwardly and fortifying the intestines inwardly. Another term for those frozen in place is that they are "rubber stamp" people. When another day rolls around, they just pull out the rubber stamp of themselves they used yesterday and smack the new calendar with it again.

7) LOW SELF-ESTEEM

Self-esteem as commonly talked about is based upon how we value what we view of ourselves. It is our sum total of all the little +'s and -'s that we have appended to ourselves at that particular moment in time. People with a + total possess what we have come to call "high" self-esteem. People with a - total possess what we have come to call "low" self-esteem. We pretty much accumulated the +'s and -'s as reflections back to us from the heavy players during our early years. They based that reflection on what they felt, valued, needed, etc., at the time. In other words, the whole thing is really a house of mirrors – illusory and fairly shaky.

The truth is we are born with healthy self-esteem and it is either supported or denied from then on. If affirmed, it flourishes, and if denied, it is covered with what the big players wanted us to be. After all, they were the keepers of the food. Healthy self-esteem is a matter of "uncovering" what is there, rather than somehow adding what isn't.

The workplace becomes the playing ground to prove to ourselves over and over that we are right about our illusory self-esteem conclusion. Few people change much about their self-esteem in the workplace. That's not the game. The game is about "being right about that" whether your self-esteem is high or low. The workplace provides many, many opportunities either way. Dysfunctional family survivors are distinguishable because they are VERY into the game.

8) COMPULSIVE BEHAVIORS

Compulsive behaviors are learned circular habits that place a person eventually into a "damned if I do" and "damned if I don't" quandary or dualism. "If I don't smoke I feel like I'll go crazy, but if I do smoke I feel unhealthy and dumb." "If I don't have a shopping frenzy I feel deprived and depressed, but when I do I feel ashamed of all the money I am spending that should go somewhere else." "If I work real hard I feel stressed and resentful, but if I don't I feel lazy and worthless." "If I drink I feel like crap about myself, but if I don't I can't relax and I miss out on all the fun." "I have to eat and love to eat my favorite foods, but when I start eating I lose control and then I feel like a big pig." "If I don't worry I feel like bad things will happen, but when I worry it rains on my whole day." And so it goes, chasing back and forth between the two options like a runner caught between the bases.

Compulsive and addictive behaviors attract us because they initially work very well. Having a few beers really does taste good, feel good, and relax us. Overdoing it while eating out once in a while is a nice respite from cooking at home, and all the new flavors and dishes are exciting. But eventually we are using excesses to escape our feelings and to get a little buzz, and we just keep doing it over and over again until we can't say "No" anymore. At this point the compulsive behavior has become more than just fun and escape, it has become a central part of our lives that we feel we cannot do without, and, at the same time, it begins to have life damaging consequences - DUIs with the alcohol, lung problems with the cigarettes, overweight problems with the food, financial problems with the gambling or shopping, blood pressure or digestive problems with the work, etc., and we still can't say "No."

I was once hired in a mental health firm because I told them I did not get behind in my paperwork. The Director said, "Oh, good, another compulsive like me, we need more people like you around here. Then things would get done!" I resigned the job before I started. If the type of person they most wanted was the kind of person they should be treating, then obviously it was not going to be a healthy place to work. Compulsive behaviors by definition are destructive. They should be intervened upon and brought to a halt while there is still a life to save. Any work environment that does not confront compulsive behaviors enables them.

CHAPTER NINE

WHY IS ABUSE HARMFUL?

This question may appear silly to ask, but not when you consider how prevalent abuse is, and has been, down through time. Millions have justified abuse, often righteously. Just think of the many clichés: "The best defense is a good offense" (and, of course, I have the right to defend myself!); "Spare the rod and spoil the child" (and nobody will like the child if it's spoiled so I'm doing it a favor!); "This hurts me worse than it does you" (it's your good fortune that you have someone willing to suffer in order to teach you such a valuable lesson!); "We must have order" (and there just is no better way to achieve this order than to punish you!). If you have read the abuse list in Appendix I, then you realize that there is practically no end to abuse. We are, like the fish, immersed in it to such a degree that we no longer notice it. Despite all the laws, commandments, morals, ethics, and poetry pleading down through the years, we still have a plethora of abuse occurring on a nearly constant basis. It seems almost legitimate to say, "Come on, let's be honest, abuse is a way of life...we just have all these little "rules" to keep it under control. Just don't get caught and it's no big deal. Don't be so naive."

Indeed, just what is so bad about abuse? Answer: It goes against the "Plan" – the plan of actualizing our "spirituality." [Note: This is not a religious conceptualization, but is, rather, a statement about individual human destiny being a natural state of lightness, sensitivity, beauty, health, and intelligent concern for self and others.]

It is proposed by some that the ultimate human-body purpose is to reach a state of consistent spirituality. If that is true, or is at least supposed to be true, it is very difficult to acquire this blissful harmonious state and participate in abusive behaviors at the same time. It is simply a law of physics that two things cannot occupy the same space at the same time. Abuse and Spirituality cannot occupy the same human at the same time, or better stated; one cannot express one's positive spiritual nature while being abusive. It is also very difficult to express one's spirituality while allowing oneself to be abused. Some saints have done this, but it is such a hazardous path that it is not recommended as a consciously chosen road to self-actualization.

Abusiveness is incongruent with human destiny. That is the reason abuse is painful. The pain is an indicator of being off the Path. It has always been this way. It probably always will be this way. It is a beautiful self-regulating system, especially when it is heeded.

"Don't ever forget, Miss Radha: To the senseless, nothing is more maddening than sense. Pala is a small island completely surrounded by twenty-nine hundred million mental cases. In the country of the insane the integrated man doesn't become King." Mr. Bahu's face was positively twinkling with Voltairean glee. "He gets lynched!"

(ISLAND, Aldous Huxley, 1962)

Remember: Just because history seems to verify that abuse is habitual doesn't make it sane or humane.

So, abuse is destructive because:

One can never be deeply, satisfyingly, healthfully, harmoniously, and genuinely human in the midst of abuse.

Most people, it seems, want a spiritual lifestyle more than anything. They started out as innocent, genuine, loving, spontaneous humans as babies and then lost these positive characteristics due to abuse. They can get them back by saying "No" to abuse in any form, by recovering from abusive patterns that have been internalized as coping mechanisms, and by learning all they can about this accepted destructive philosophy of nihilism.

Relationships of Abuse Forms

The potential negative consequence of all abuse/neglect is a rupture in the victim's relationship with his/her pristine self. This creates a dynamic in which all forms of abuse/neglect can ultimately result in *spiritual abuse* – damaging the primary and foundational relationship with self. This explains why sexual abuse often creates the deepest damage in the individual.

Sexual abuse interferes directly with our identity because primarily we identify ourselves by our gender. The first thing everyone wants to know when a newborn arrives is its gender. This is so that "it" can be related to as an individual identity. The very foundation of personality formation rests upon gender in our society. Sexual abuse casts shame and doubt upon the manner by which the victim relates with his/her own core personality orientation. This can have pervasive and long-term damaging consequences for the victim in all future relationships.

Likewise, emotional abuse is very powerful because emotions are both physical and mental and provide the psychosomatic link between mind and body. Thus, emotional abuse is two-pronged and affects all parts of the victim's world very quickly.

Notes:

A) See suggestions for utilizing the Classification System of Child Abuse and Neglect (**CSCAN**) in Appendix I and a suggested reporting system for more effective record keeping and research beginning on page 84.

B) A suggested Classification System of Abuse and Neglect of Adults (**CSANA**) - which is actually somewhat beyond the scope of this book - is included in Appendix II. It is included to graphically demonstrate the long-term effects of abuse and neglect in children. In other words, it makes the point that acts of abuse and neglect do not end upon the physical healing of wounds in the child, but become the child's personal legacy into adulthood.

C) A special case of social abuse, Triangulation, is included in Appendix III because of its prevalence as a vehicle for various other forms of abuse.

D) Appendices II and III are included to provide the reader some insight into how adults in their daily lives perpetuate what was done unto them as children, i.e., the various means of exhibiting the process addiction to abuse.

CHAPTER TEN

Value and Utilization of the
CLASSIFICATION SYSTEM OF CHILD ABUSE AND NEGLECT (CSCAN)

The Value of a Nomenclature

The overall benefit of a nomenclature, such as the Classification System of Child Abuse and Neglect (CSCAN) located in Appendix I, may be that it provides, for the first time, substantiated evidence of the potential impact of specific child-raising behaviors. This may provide, again for the first time, an opportunity to determine the "cost-effectiveness" of any specific behavior. Once an agreed upon nomenclature and its universal acceptance can be established, a centralized database of accumulated research can then be created. This database would generate centralized findings of cause-effect studies, cost-effectively interpret those findings, and distribute them to professionals and the public alike. Legislators, parents, and all the professionals in between would have the hard figures necessary to make accurate judgements about specific child treatment behaviors.

I suggest that schools, social welfare agencies, health care professionals, and legal branches of our government begin to dialogue about the institution of such a system as **CSCAN** for these very reasons. I further suggest a convenient reporting, or concise shorthand method of recording such data. This will be helpful in establishing databases and eventually accurately referencing long-term effects of specific forms of abuse and neglect.

[Casual readers may wish to skip the next three pages.]

A Notation and Reporting System of Abuse & Neglect

A classification system such as CSCAN can be conveniently encoded into a tri-part alphanumerical phrase that denotes the category of abuse and the specific form of abuse/neglect (the core of the alphanumeric phrase), the age(s) of the victim at the time of abuse/neglect and frequency of the abuse/neglect (the pretext of the alphanumeric phrase), and the perpetrator(s) (the posttext of the alphanumeric phrase), if applicable.

Key:

a) The pretext appears as a decimal. The first number in the pretext is the age(s) of the person during abusive/neglectful episodes, and the number after the decimal point in the pretext is frequency: 1 = one occurrence only; 2 = occasional occurrences; 3 = frequent occurrences; ? = undetermined.

b) The middle code after the double slash // is a prefix denoting the general form of abuse/neglect, and a number defining the specific type.

c) The posttext denotes the identity of the abuser, if ascertained, and a ? if not.

Examples:

<u>3.1 // PA.10 // father</u> At the age of 3 there was one occurrence when the father struck the child with an object.

<u>12-15.3 // SA.2 // aunt</u> Between the ages of 12 and 15 the aunt sexually fondled the child on a frequent basis.

<u>19.1 // ASAPA.1 // self</u> At the age of 19 this person self-inflicted physical injury once. [The ASA in front of the core PA represents Adult Self Abuse, in this case physical abuse (PA).]

0-P.3 // EN.2 // parents This child has been perpetually emotionally neglected since birth by both parents. [The P in the pretext stands for *up to the Present*.]

5-12.2 // PN.2.c // ? This child, between the ages of 5 and 12, occasionally was without proper clothing. [There is a *?* posttext denotation since those that were supposed to be responsible caregivers were unidentifiable. Perhaps the child was kidnapped, parents both died or were missing, or the child was in a war torn country during this time.]

This reporting system needs field trials for debugging purposes, much as the DSM-III went through before its final formulation back in the 80's. It appears well worth it when one considers that it will be more precise and efficient in terms of recordkeeping and research. Again, it may well provide the vehicle for hard data needed to legislatively put an end to the rampant ravaging of our greatest natural resource, our children.

> It is important to remember that, psychologically speaking, abuse & neglect are subjectively validated experiences. Any legal proceedings for affixing culpability are utilized only to objectify what the victim has known since the moment of violation.

NOTES:

On using the Appendices

Read over **Appendix II**. You may be surprised at just how many forms of abuse exist in adult person-to-person relationships.

Read **Appendix III** and reflect upon its implications in your life and/or your present day family's life and/or your workplace life. What would it be like if people consciously made an effort to refrain from triangulation in each of these settings?

Copy both assessment instruments in **Appendix IV**, then fill them out for your family of origin and for your present day family. This will give you a fairly good profile of not only your abuse/neglect origins, but also your current relationship to them.

<u>On support groups</u>

After completing the book and the appendices you may wish to consult some of the sources in the Bibliography. If you are interested in a support group in your area you may contact the American Self-Help Clearinghouse at these electronic addresses:
Telephone: 201/625-9053 or CompuServe: 70275,1003
or by mail:
American Self-Help Clearinghouse
Saint Clares-Riverside Medical Center
25 Pocono Road
Denville, NJ 07834
or:
If there is no dysfunctional family survivor support group in your area and you would like guidance in starting one, you may order a <u>free</u> **12-Step Starter Packet** from:

Three Blue Herons Publishing, Inc.
P.O. Box 463
Fond du Lac, Wisconsin 54936-0463

Please enclose a check or M.O. for $5 to cover s/h and postage.

APPENDIX I

CLASSIFICATION SYSTEM OF CHILD ABUSE AND NEGLECT (CSCAN)

The compilation that makes up **CSCAN** is derived from numerous client files and many other sources, including those listed at the end of this book.

Note: So-called "verbal abuse" is not included as a separate category in **CSCAN** because, technically, words are tools or methods of conveyance of other forms of abuse. Words are often used to create mental and emotional abuse. Yelling "Fire!" in a crowded restaurant would be a verbal vehicle for physical abuse. Sexual abuse can also be verbally transmitted. For example, one can denigrate a person sexually by ridiculing his or her genitalia.

CLASSIFICATION SYSTEM OF CHILD ABUSE AND NEGLECT (CSCAN)

PHYSICAL ABUSE **(PA)**

PA.___

01. Deliberate attempted murder
02. Slapping with the hand (not spanking)
03. Shaking with rapid movement
04. Scratching with the fingers
05. Pinching with the fingers
06. Squeezing painfully
07. Hitting with the fist
08. Spanking
09. Pulling hair
10. Beating with objects, (boards, sticks, belts, kitchen utensils, yardsticks, electric cords, shovels, fan belts, hoses, etc.)
11. Throwing
12. Shoving
13. Slamming against walls or objects
14. Utilizing temperature extremes:

a. burning

b. scalding

c. freezing

15. Forcing of food
16. Forcing of water
17. Forcing of objects into orifices (does not include sexual abuse)
18. Utilizing objects to pinch, poke or scratch
19. Painful tickling
20. Overworking

PHYSICAL NEGLECT **(PN)**

PN.___

01. Attempted murder via willful preoccupation (allowing a person to enter a life-threatening situation with the intent he/she will be fatally injured)
02. Lack of essentials:

a. food

b. water

c. clothing

d. shelter

03. Leaving the child alone in age-inappropriate ways
04. Leaving a child who is too young in charge of others
05. Failure to provide medical care
06. Allowing or encouraging the use of alcohol and/or other drugs
07. Failure to protect the child from the abuse of others
08. Failure to protect the child from the abuse of the spouse

EMOTIONAL ABUSE **(EA)**

EA.___

01. Double binds (a deliberately perpetrated predicament where all choices given the child are negative ones)
02. Projection and transfer of adult problems onto the child (scapegoating)
03. Alterations of child's reality (lying) e.g."Dad's not drunk, he's just tired."
04. Overprotecting (does not healthfully allow child to experience consequences of its own actions)
05. Enmeshment, or smothering with apparent affection (living through the child)
06. Preventing the child from learning appropriate developmental tasks (trust; autonomy; initiative; industry; etc.)
07. Double messages, e.g., "Of course, I love you, dear." (said as Mom tenses up and grimaces); "I love you just as you are, you just need to change a couple of traits."; "I love spending time with you, I just have to run right now."; etc.
08. Not acknowledging that abuse or neglect has taken place

09. Using child for personal gain, e.g., financial profit, holding on to a spouse, providing a sense of meaning for the parent, etc.

EMOTIONAL NEGLECT **(EN)**

EN.___

01. Desertion, abandonment
02. Failure to nurture, care for or love the child
03. Failure to provide structure or set limits
04. Not listening to, hearing or believing the child
05. Expecting the child to provide unreasonable emotional nurturing to adults instead of receiving it
06. Deliberately withdrawing or withholding love
07. Caregivers not being emotionally present due to:
    a. mental illness
    b. chemical dependency
    c. depression
    d. compulsivity in themselves
    e. compulsivity in the family environment
    f. extended physical illness
08. Excessive guilting (dwelling on mistakes)

09. Excessive shaming (characterizing the child as flawed, defective, a "mistake," or at fault for existing)
10. Sarcasm (sideways anger)
11. Inflicting unreasonable fear
12. Minimizing the child's emotions ("You shouldn't feel sad, angry, afraid, happy, etc.")

MENTAL ABUSE **(MA)**

MA___

01. Excessive blaming (overloaded with criticism)
02. Degrading
03. Name calling
04. Put-downs by comparisons
05. Excessive teasing
06. Making fun of, laughing at, belittling
07. Nagging or haranguing
08. Screaming
09. Verbal assault (frequent "jackhammer" barrages of words)
10. Manipulating, deceiving, tricking (deliberate misleading)
11. Betraying

12. Cruelty
13. Intimidating, threatening, bullying
14. Controlling or overpowering
15. Not taking child's thoughts seriously
16. Put-downs via patronizing
17. Discrediting (not giving credit where it is due)
18. Disapproving of child's individuality
19. Making light of or minimizing wants, needs
20. Raising hopes falsely, breaking promises
21. Responding inconsistently or arbitrarily
22. Making vague demands
23. Saying "If only you were...[better or different]"
24. Denigrated because of gender, ethnic, religious or racial differences

MENTAL NEGLECT **(MN)**

MN.___

01. Lack of communication skills development
02. Lack of praise or encouragement to develop intellectually
03. Undereducation
04. Lack of affirmation regarding uniqueness

SEXUAL ABUSE (SA)

SA.___

01. Forced rape
02. Fondling, inappropriate touching
03. Sexual harassment, innuendoes, jokes, comments
04. Leering
05. Exposing self to
06. Masturbating in front of
07. Mutual masturbation
08. Oral sex
09. Anal sex
10. Intercourse
11. Penetration with fingers
12. Penetration with objects
13. Stripping/exposing
14. Sexual punishments
15. Inappropriate or excessive enemas
16. Pornography: taking inappropriate pictures and/or forcing the child to watch
17. Coercing children to have sex with each other
18. Forced sexual activity with animals

19. Inappropriate invasion of bathroom/bedroom privacy

SEXUAL NEGLECT **(SN)**

SN.___

01. Failure to educate children concerning healthy sexual limits and boundaries
02. Failure to educate children concerning menstruation, conception, pregnancy, birth control, sexually transmitted diseases, etc.
03. Failure to help children differentiate intimacy issues from sexual issues
04. Failure to help children develop positive self-esteem regarding their sexual selves

VICARIOUS ABUSE **(VA)**

VA.

A special case of abuse, in which the victim is part of a family or other system in which someone else is abused in some way. The witnessing of abuse (PA, EA, MA, SA) can be just as damaging as being the actual recipient of the abuse.

Important Note: Please continue to dialogue with us at the Institute for Transformational Studies concerning your successful utilization of and/or suggested modifications to the CSCAN and CSANA systems. You will become part of our ongoing database, and as further versions of the classification systems are realized, you will be notified.

Feedback address:

INSTITUTE FOR TRANSFORMATIONAL STUDIES
P.O. Box 1181
Fond du Lac, WI 54936-1181

The latest version of CSCAN or CSANA assessment forms are available from:

THREE BLUE HERONS PUBLISHING, INC.
P. O. Box 463
Fond du Lac, WI 54936-0463

$9.95 for a pad of 25 sheets on color-coded paper + **$3 s/h** per order of 5 pads or less. Specify which form. Each sheet includes all current CSCAN or CSANA categories and denotations in a checklist format.

APPENDIX II

CLASSIFICATION SYSTEM OF ABUSE AND NEGLECT OF ADULTS (CSANA)

ADULT FORMS OF ABUSE AND NEGLECT

Many childhood forms of abuse are also applicable to adults. In addition to those, some forms that are listed below are commonly found only in the adult stages of life. If one is using a denotation system it would be clarifying to include **A_S-A** for Adult [form] Self Abuse, or **A_** for Adult Abuse in the classification core (see pages 90-92).

In the Classification System of Abuse & Neglect of Adults (CSANA) self-neglect is included under the Self-Abuse categories.)

ADULT SELF-ABUSE(A_S-A)/ADULT ABUSE(A)

ADULT PHYSICAL SELF-ABUSE **(APS-A)**

APS-A.___

01. Self-mutilation with razors or knives
02. Skin-gouging
03. Tattoos
04. Nail-biting
05. Lack of proper exercise
06. Over-exercising
07. Chronic insufficient rest or overexertion
08. Addiction (physical dependency upon) to:
    a. alcohol
    b. other mood altering chemicals
    c. nicotine
09. Compulsive behaviors:
    a. Work
    b. Sex
    c. Gambling
    d. Religion
    e. Food:

i. Overeating
ii. Undereating
iii. Bulimia

f. Spending
g. Sports
h. Television-viewing
i. Hoarding
j. Inappropriate collecting
k. Money
l. Miserliness
m. Extremely dependent relationships

10. Allowing others to inflict pain in any form
11. Not availing oneself of proper medical attention

ADULT PHYSICAL ABUSE **(APA)**

APA.___

01. Deliberate attempted murder
02. Slapping with the hand (not spanking)
03. Shaking with rapid movement
04. Scratching with the fingers
05. Pinching with the fingers

06. Squeezing painfully
07. Hitting with the fist
08. Spanking
09. Pulling hair
10. Beating with objects, (boards, sticks, etc.)
11. Throwing
12. Shoving
13. Slamming against walls or objects
14. Utilizing temperature extremes:
    __a. burning
    __b. scalding
    __c. freezing
15. Forcing of food
16. Forcing of water
17. Forcing of objects into orifices (doesn't include sexual abuse)
18. Utilizing objects to pinch, poke or scratch
19. Painful tickling
20. Overworking

ADULT MENTAL SELF-ABUSE **(AMS-A)**

AMS-A.___

01. Neglecting spiritual nourishment
02. Refraining from growth/inner-healing opportunities
03. Unrealistic self-expectations
04. Undermining dignity of self
05. Continually escaping the present moment
06. Self-condemning inner voices

ADULT MENTAL ABUSE **(AMA)**

AMA.___

01. Excessive blaming (overloaded with criticism)
02. Degrading
03. Name calling
04. Put-downs by comparisons
05. Excessive teasing
06. Making fun of, laughing at, belittling
07. Nagging or haranguing
08. Screaming

09. Verbal assault ("jack-hammer" word barrages)
10. Manipulating, deceiving, tricking (deliberate misleading)
11. Betraying
12. Cruelty
13. Intimidating, threatening, bullying
14. Controlling or overpowering
15. Not taking thoughts seriously
16. Put-downs via patronizing
17. Discrediting (not giving credit where it is due)
18. Disapproving of individuality
19. Making light of or minimizing wants, needs
20. Raising hopes falsely, breaking promises
21. Responding inconsistently or arbitrarily
22. Making vague demands
23. Saying "If only you were...[better or different]"
24. Denigrated because of gender, ethnic, religious, class or racial differences
25. Telephone abuse
26. Unsupported in sickness, injury or pregnancy
27. Abandoned in dangerous places
28. Workplace abuse - personal harassment

29. Workplace abuse - environmental issues, e.g., overwork, undue stress, poor working conditions)

ADULT EMOTIONAL SELF-ABUSE **(AES-A)**

AES-A.___

01. Suppressing emotions
02. Denial of abuse
03. Failure to nurture spontaneity and/or creativity
04. Fostering low self-esteem
05. Expecting oneself to compensate for or accommodate another's irrational mood swings

ADULT EMOTIONAL ABUSE **(AEA)**

AEA.___

01. Double binds (a deliberately perpetrated predicament where all choices given are negative ones)
02. Projection and transfer of problems onto another (scapegoating)

03. Alteration of reality (lying)
04. Overprotecting (does not healthfully allow one to experience consequences of own actions)
05. Enmeshment, or smothering with apparent affection (living through the other person)
06. Preventing from learning or developing
07. Double messages, "I love you just as you are, you just need to change a couple of traits."; etc.
08. Not acknowledging that abuse or neglect has taken place
09. Using a person for personal gain, e.g., financial profit, providing a sense of meaning, etc.

ADULT SEXUAL SELF-ABUSE **(ASS-A)**

ASS-A.___

01. Exposing self to sexually transmitted diseases
02. Allowing self to be demoralizingly sexually used
03. Indulging obsessive sexual thoughts or behaviors

ADULT SEXUAL ABUSE **(ASA)**

ASA.___

[Must be non-consensual to classify as abusive]

01. Forced rape
02. Fondling, inappropriate touching
03. Sexual harassment, innuendoes, jokes, comments
04. Leering
05. Exposing self to
06. Masturbating in front of
07. Mutual masturbation
08. Oral sex
09. Anal sex
10. Coerced intercourse
11. Penetration with fingers
12. Penetration with objects
13. Stripping/exposing
14. Sexual punishments
15. Inappropriate or excessive enemas
16. Pornography: taking inappropriate pictures and/or forcing one to watch
17. Coercing one into sexual activity with another

18. Forced sexual activity with animals
19. Inappropriate invasion of sexual privacy
20. Coerced sex by emotional blackmail
21. Withholding sex to manipulate
22. Affairs by partner
23. Continual flirting by partner

ADULT FINANCIAL SELF-ABUSE **(AFS-A)**

AFS-A.___

01. Spending beyond means
02. Excessive gambling
03. Choosing to remain ignorant regarding money matters
04. Allowing another to create financial difficulties
05. Miserliness

ADULT FINANCIAL ABUSE **(AFA)**

AFA.___

01. Engendering self-diminishment of another person through bribery

02. Blackmail
03. Raping another financially (destructive competition)
04. Theft
05. Borrowing without repaying
06. Trickery - con games - fraud
07. Mishandling of investments through avoidable ignorance
08. Misrepresentation of item/event value

APPENDIX III

TRIANGULATION

This section is included because it clearly defines a frequently socialized pattern of abuse, i.e., it is too important not to include. Triangulation serves as a great example of just how ordinary and socially acceptable certain forms of abuse and neglect have becom, signifying that the process of acclimation is not always beneficial. We extend a warm thanks to Marsha Utain and Barb Oliver for the clarity which they have bring to this common pattern of toxic human interaction.

[The following section is adapted, modified and reprinted from SCREAM LOUDER *by Marsha Utain and Barbara Oliver, 1989,* with the permission of the publisher: Health Communications, Inc., Deerfield Beach, FL.]

TRIANGULATION

A Common and Complex Form of Social Abuse

The Drama Triangle is the representation of a complex interactional process involving the three participating roles of Victim, Persecutor and Rescuer. The Triangle is based on blame and guilt and is put into operation whenever any type of lie or denial occurs. Without blame, guilt or lies, there would be no Drama Triangle and no chaos. Instead there would be healthy responsible relationships based on honest and clear communications.

Victim

The Victim position is the key role in the Triangle because it is the position around which the others revolve. People operating in the Victim position take no responsibility for their actions or feelings. They truly believe that they are life's "fall guys," and that everyone in the world is "doing it to them." They continually look for someone or something else to blame for things not working in their lives. Victims can frequently be identified by their usage of such language as: "Everyone, anyone does it to me," "you/they (the government, mother, father, boss, spouse, children, etc.) do it to me," "poor me."

There are two basic types of victims: The Pathetic Victim, and the Angry Victim. The Pathetic Victim plays the pity ploy, using woeful "poor me" looks and the desolate language of self-pity, while the Angry Victim pretends to be powerful, using angry "I won't let you do it to me," "Look what you did to me," or "You're bad" types of language.

Both types of Victim are looking for someone to blame for the emotions that they are having and for their lives not working. In addition, they are looking for a Rescuer, someone they can "hook" into taking care of them and their responsibilities.

Rescuer

As any recovering co-alcoholic knows, the role of the Rescuer is a highly addictive role because it is the position of the "Good Guy." Because of the way most people are raised, whenever they feel guilty they have learned to get out of the guilt by moving into the Rescuer "Good Guy" position. People do not like to be labeled "Bad Guys" so they actively seek the position of Rescuer and, because it affords them some relief from pain, they become addicted to it.

We are raised from birth to believe that we must be "good." We are trained by the standards of our parents, churches and society that in order to be "good" we must take care of other people physically, emotionally or spiritually, even at the cost of our own being. We are drilled with the idea that to take care of oneself is to be selfish which is, of course, bad. Therefore, when the Victim approaches us with blame or tales of woe, we are already prime targets for the manipulative hook of guilt. We already believe that we should take care of other people's problems, and that if we do not, we are "bad". Because we do not wish to be cast in the "Bad Guy" Persecutor role, we jump in to rescue the Victim, even when it is not in our best interests.

If a child did not do what the parent wanted, then the child was labeled "bad" and cast in the role of the Persecutor. Taking the position of Rescuer, therefore, affords a person some relief from guilt and gives the person the opportunity to pretend that they are acting unselfishly and for someone else's good. This creates the momentary high that makes the

Rescuer position addictive. The Rescuer does not realize that they are motivated by selfish reasons. They just do not want to feel like or appear to be a "bad" person.

There is another important point to understand about Rescuers in the Drama Triangle. Because of the very nature of the Triangle, Rescuers must have a Victim, someone to take care of, someone to control, someone, who by their very need, makes the rescuer feel good. When people are co-dependent and therefore addicted to the Rescuer role, they will find that they actually have a need to rescue. In order to fill that need, they need a Victim that they can "help." If there isn't one available the Rescuer will attempt to create one.

In general, Rescuers need to be needed, and they need to be in control and be right, no matter what the cost. Being in control and being right allows the Rescuer to avoid dealing with their own emotions or discomfort. In all addictions the addictive substance or behavior (in this case Rescuing) is used by the addict to avoid feelings.

Persecutor

The role of the Persecutor is the role of the "Bad Guy," the villain. It is the one role that few people consciously choose as their starting place in the Triangle. In fact, it is the role that keeps the Triangle going because people in the Triangle are attempting to avoid this position by moving into the Rescuer role or by perceiving themselves as Victims. No one likes to see themselves as the "Bad Guy." Even convicted felons want to be seen as the Victims of society, rather than society's Persecutors. The Persecutor role is the one that Victims use, along with blame, to maneuver others into rescuing them. What makes the Persecutor position very interesting is the fact that once you are in the Triangle and you decide to leave it, you must leave from this position. In other words, when you remove yourself from playing the Triangle, anyone still playing will perceive you as the Persecutor.

Positioning, Maneuvering And Rules in the Triangle

A number of key points to consider remembering:

1. **The Triangle is based on lies.** Tell a lie to yourself or someone else, whether it is a lie about data or a lie about your emotions or your experience, and you move immediately into the Triangle and the addictive process.

2. **All shoulds are a lie**, therefore, shoulds will throw you into the Triangle. (An important piece of your healing process is learning how to go about getting your needs and wants met after you learn to distinguish them from your 'shoulds' or the things that other people have told you are your needs.)

3. **All positions in the Triangle cause pain.** No matter what position you are in at any given moment in the Triangle, you will be in some form of discomfort or pain.

4. **There is no power in the Triangle.** When you are in the Triangle, you are operating from powerlessness and irresponsibility no matter what position you are playing.

5. **Everyone has a favorite starting position** which is usually either the Rescuer or the Victim. Few people choose Persecutor as a starting position.

6. **Once you are hooked into the Triangle, you will end up playing all the positions, whether you like it or not,** because of the nature of the Triangle. You may perceive yourself as a Rescuer who wound up as someone's Victim while, at the same time, that person perceives you as the Persecutor.

7. **Guilt is the experience that hooks you into the Triangle,** and therefore you need to learn a few points about guilt:

a. Guilt is a signal that someone is pulling you into the Triangle.

b. In order to stay out of the Triangle you need to learn to give yourself permission to feel guilty without acting on that guilt. In other words, do not let the guilt push you into the Rescuer position.

c. Learn to sit with the guilt and be uncomfortable. This particular type of guilt is not the same as that of being out of integrity with yourself by breaking a rule, moral or law.

8. **The "escape hatch" out of the Triangle is located at the Persecutor position.** Telling the truth and feeling your emotions opens the escape hatch out of the Triangle. In other words, in order to leave the Triangle or, for that matter, to stay out of it, you have to be willing for others (the Victims or the other Rescuers) to perceive you as the "Bad Guy" and then go through whatever emotions surface as a result of their perception. This does not mean that you **are** the "Bad Guy;" it just means that others choose to see you that way. If you are not willing to be seen as a Persecutor, you will get hooked into rescuing and keep yourself in the Triangle. If you are already in the Triangle and wish to leave, you have to be willing for the others in the Triangle to see you as the Persecutor.

9. **You can play the Triangle alone with yourself.** (Once you have been raised in a dysfunctional family, you do not need anyone else to push you into the Triangle.)
a. The way you play the Triangle by yourself is by listening to the negative voice inside your head that beats you up, "puts you down" and constantly "shoulds on you."

b. Remember, 'shoulds' are a lie. They have nothing to do with who you are. They are someone else's interpretation of what to do and what is good.
c. When you play the Triangle with yourself, your should-er will persecute you so that you will feel like the Victim. At the same time you will be feeling guilty. This will trigger the belief that you are the Persecutor. The guilt will drive you to "rescue" someone (or some situation), even when no one, except you, is there attempting to manipulate you into the Rescuer position.

10. **When you actively participate in a relationship with someone who lives in the Triangle, you must be very careful of the hooks.** It is difficult to be around people who constantly operate in the Triangle and not get hooked in yourself, especially if your personal boundaries are not clear and you have not learned to recognize the Triangle.

11. **Your internalized should-er is also the voice that pushes you into the Triangle when others around you are already in and attempting to hook you.** The Should-er is the false-self, the part that is actually someone else you believe is you. It is controlling, negative, rigid, perfectionistic and

righteous. Without that part of you operating, you would not participate in the Triangle.

12. **Being in the Triangle is not being alive; it is a living death.** It is a life of pain, inauthenticity, and lack of love and acceptance.

13. **Suicide is the ultimate Victim act, the ultimate act of self-pity.** When the Victim perceives they cannot get anyone to come to the rescue anymore, and they do not have the courage to seek new alternatives, they may turn to suicide.

14. **Telling the truth and experiencing your emotions is the only way out of the Triangle.** To do that you have to learn to know and define your boundaries and take care of responsibility for recognizing, experiencing, expressing and completing your emotions.

Avoiding the Triangle

To stay out of the Triangle, learn to tell the truth about what emotions you are feeling and take responsibility for them. Remember that no one else is responsible for your emotions.

No one else can fix them for you or change them for you. People may support you in experiencing them, but ultimately no one but you can complete and release your emotions.

Frequently dysfunctional families are so repressive you cannot identify certain emotions or distinguish them from other types of experiences. When you: a) tell the truth about what you are feeling; b) no longer take on the guilt that others try to place on you; and, c) are willing to feel the fear and sadness when being accused of being the Persecutor by people who stay in the Triangle, you will step out of the chaos in your life. By being responsible for acknowledging and experiencing your emotions, you are also being responsible for your addictive process.

When you are further along in your healing process, you will be able to recognize your various emotions. Then you will begin to express them to others in order to get further in touch with the emotions and not as an attempt to make someone else responsible for them. Remember: This is a process, and you may slide back and forth along the denial<=>acceptance continuum until you are truly and completely in touch with your emotions.

APPENDIX IV

ASSESSMENT FORMS

1. Family of Origin Health Continuum & Questionnaire

2. Personal Health Continuum & Questionnaire

FAMILY AND PERSONAL ASSESSMENT

The Family of Origin Health Continuum & Questionnaire and the Personal Health Continuum & Questionnaire are designed to help you gain personal understanding of the material in the book and to discover how you have been affected by it. It is important to both our own development and the way we interact with others personally and professionally to do this for ourselves. Take your time, refer to the pages noted under each item for clarification, and then, after completing the assessment portion, answer the questions. You may find this discomforting, so please remember to breathe.

A common question is, "At what point in historical time should I view my family for the purposes of assessment?" Whichever perspective has the most significance for you. Some people have an overall perspective of their family of origin and respond to the questionnaire as if constructing a representational collage. Other people do the questionnaire from several historical perspectives, e.g. one before a parent sobered up and one for after, or one before Mom and Dad divorced and one after, etc.

FAMILY HEALTH CONTINUUM

Honestly consider <u>your family of origin.</u> Circle the number that accurately reflects your perception regarding each area during your childhood (whatever "age" you choose).

Abuse/Neglect	Never	. . . .		Daily	*Comments:*
a. physical abuse (pg. 99)	0	1	2	3	4
b. physical neglect (pg. 100)	0	1	2	3	4
c. emotional abuse (pg. 102)	0	1	2	3	4
d. emotional neglect (pg. 103)	0	1	2	3	4
e. mental abuse (pg. 104)	0	1	2	3	4
f. mental neglect (pg. 106)	0	1	2	3	4
g. sexual abuse (pg. 107)	0	1	2	3	4
h. sexual neglect (pg. 108)	0	1	2	3	4
i. vicarious abuse (pg. 108)	0	1	2	3	4
2. perfectionism (godlike, always right caregiver)	0	1	2	3	4
3. rigid rules/beliefs (laws more important than people)	0	1	2	3	4
4. no talk rule (a family is as sick as its secrets)	0	1	2	3	4

5. can't identify or	0	1	2	3	4
express all emotions (learn not to feel)					
6. triangulation	0	1	2	3	4
7. spontaneity	0	1	2	3	4
discouraged (too threatening)					
8. high tolerance for	0	1	2	3	4
pain or inappropriate behavior					
9. enmeshment:					
Type A	0	1	2	3	4
(No boundaries in family)					
Type B	0	1	2	3	4
(Psycho-emotionally and/or physically isolated individuals within the home)					

Answer the following questions.

1. What does this tell you about your family?

2. What parts of this would you like to change?

3. How do you think this has affected your outlook on life regarding others, yourself, the world in general?

4. What behaviors from your family of origin do you wish to retain? Explain why.

5. Would the continuum chart be different if it were done for each parent individually?

PERSONAL HEALTH CONTINUUM

Honestly consider yourself. Circle the number that accurately reflects your perception of your present day behavior, both dispensing and receiving abuse/neglect.

Abuse/Neglect	Never . . . . Daily					*Comments:*
a. physical abuse (pgs. 99, 113-115)	0	1	2	3	4	
b. physical neglect (pg. 100)	0	1	2	3	4	
c. emotional abuse (pgs. 102 & 118-119)	0	1	2	3	4	
d. emotional neglect (pg. 103)	0	1	2	3	4	
e. mental abuse (pgs. 104 & 116-118)	0	1	2	3	4	
f. mental neglect (pg. 106)	0	1	2	3	4	
g. sexual abuse (pages 107 & 119-121)	0	1	2	3	4	
h. sexual neglect (pg. 108)	0	1	2	3	4	
i. vicarious abuse (pg. 108)	0	1	2	3	4	
2. perfectionism (godlike, always right caregiver)	0	1	2	3	4	
3. rigid rules/beliefs (laws more important than people)	0	1	2	3	4	
4. no talk rule (a family is as sick as its secrets)	0	1	2	3	4	

5. can't identify or 0 1 2 3 4
express all emotions (learn not to feel)
6. triangulation 0 1 2 3 4
7. spontaneity 0 1 2 3 4
discouraged (too threatening)
8. high tolerance for 0 1 2 3 4
pain or inappropriate behavior
9. enmeshment:
Type A 0 1 2 3 4
(No boundaries in family)
Type B 0 1 2 3 4
(Psycho-emotionally and/or physically isolated individuals within the home)

Answer the following questions.

1. What does this tell you about yourself?

2. What parts of this would you like to change?

3. How do you think this is affecting your outlook on life regarding others, yourself, the world in general?

4. What behaviors from your family of origin are you retaining? Is it in your best interests to continue these behaviors?

5. Do you believe you can change the behaviors you need to without external assistance and support?

BIBLIOGRAPHY & READINGS

Adult Children of Abusive Parents
Steven Farmer. Lowell House Legacy. 1989.

1992 Child Abuse and Neglect Report
Bureau for Children, Youth and Families, Division of Community Services, Wisconsin Department of Health and Social Services. Madison, WI. 1992.

A Coordinated Response to Child Abuse and Neglect: A Basic Manual
U.S. Department of Health and Human Services, Administration for Children and Families. DHHS Publication No. (ACF) 92-30362. McLean, VA: The Circle, Inc. 1992.

Adult Children: The Secrets of Dysfunctional Families
John C. Friel, Ph.D and Linda Friel. Health Communications, Inc. 1988.

Bradshaw on: The Family
John Bradshaw. Health Communications, Inc. 1988.

Broken Toys, Broken Dreams
Terry Kellogg. Brat Publishing. 1990.

Children of Trauma
Jane Middleton-Moz. Health Communications, Inc. 1989.

Co-Dependence: Healing The Human Condition
Charles L. Whitfield, M.D., Health Communications, Inc. 1991.

Defining Child Abuse
Jeanne Giovannoni & Rosina Becerra. The Free Press Macmillan Publishing Co., Inc. 1979.

Drama of the Gifted Child, The
Alice Miller. Basic Books, Inc. 1981.

Facing Shame: Families in Recovery
Merle A. Fossum and Marilyn J. Mason. W.W. Norton and Company. 1986.

For Your Own Good
Alice Miller. Farrar Straus Giroux. 1988.

A Gift To Myself
Charles L. Whitfield. Health Communications, Inc. 1990.

Grandchildren of Alcoholics
Ann W. Smith. Health Communications, Inc. 1988.

Healing the Child Within
Charles L. Whitfield, M.D. Health Communications, Inc. 1984.

Healing the Shame that Binds You
John Bradshaw. Health Communications, Inc. 1988.

Healing your Sexual Self
Janet G. Woititz. Health Communications, Inc. 1989.

Physical and Sexual Abuse of Children: Causes and Treatment
David R. Walters. Indiana University Press. 1975.

Self-Help Sourcebook...Finding and Forming Mutual Aid Self-Help Groups (4th ed.)
Barbara White & Edward Madara, editors. Denville, NJ: St. Clares-Riverside Medical Center. 1992.

Soul Survivors
J. Patrick Gannon. Prentice Hall Press. 1989.

Toxic Parents - Overcoming Their Hurtful Legacy and Reclaiming Your Life
Dr. Susan Forward. Bantam. 1989.

Treatment of Adult Survivors of Childhood Abuse
Eliana Gil. Launch Press. 1988.

Victims No Longer
Mike Lew. Perennial Press. 1990

The Wounded Male
Steven Farmer. Bantam Books. 1991.

~~~~~~

You are encouraged to participate in Dr. Dallmann-Jones' live Psychotechnology Seminars offered in locations around the globe. Please write for a schedule of his appearances, or for information on sponsoring a workshop.

~~~~~~

INSTITUTE for TRANSFORMATIONAL STUDIES
P.O. Box 1181 Fond du Lac, WI 54936-1181

Mission: *The Institute exists to research, develop and produce vehicles for transforming knowledge into productive intelligence for the betterment of humankind.* To this end, empowering and rejuvenating workshops, seminars, in-services, trainings, video- and audio-tapes, and personal intensives are available.

Gillette Manor

The Institute for Transformational Studies is housed in a restored *ante bellum* Victorian home located in Fond du Lac, Wisconsin, on land purchased from the Winnebago Tribe in 1834. It is the site of the WINDOORS Training (see pg. 153) and private 3 - 6 day personal intensives with Dr. Dallmann-Jones. The intensives include journaling, reflection, one-on-one educational sessions, massage, and vegetarian meals. The relaxing atmosphere of the Gillette Manor's private suite includes a private entrance, bath, and sun porch. Advance reservations required. Call 414-921-0820.

PRODUCTS

NEW Book Release! The ***PHOENIX FLIGHT MANUAL...Rising Above The Ashes of Ordinary Existence*** by Anthony S. Dallmann-Jones, Ph.D. A major contribution to the self-help field, wherein the latest quantum physical and psychological science is translated into easily applied everyday language. Includes case studies of people who have used the Phoenix Solution to lose weight, lower golf scores, reduce stress, cure illness, solve relationship problems, and change moods at will. The ultimate book for those interested in true empowerment. (208 pp. paperback ISBN# 1-881952-49-5) Only $14.95!

Dysfunctional Family Survivor Dynamics **Video-tape - Only $29.95** (77 minutes)
An interview with Dr. Anthony Dallmann-Jones, former executive director of The National Association of Dysfunctional Family Survivors. Clearly delineates the psychodynamics of abuse/neglect that give rise to the eight characteristics of the Dysfunctional Family Survivor Syndrome. Should be required viewing for every service professional!

Self-Esteem for Survivors **Video-tape - Only $29.95** (70 minutes)
Dr. Anthony S. Dallmann-Jones offers an innovative approach with a specific and practical program for discovering healthy self-esteem. Very powerful!

Stress Management **Audio-tape - Only $10** (90 minutes)
A 5-element guided meditation narrated by Dr. Anthony Dallmann-Jones at Calfrin Waterfall in Door County, Wisconsin. The second side is 45 minutes of continuous ocean and surf sounds for use as a backdrop for practicing the 5 elements, or for just relaxing.

Dysfunctional Family Dynamics in The Classroom
Video-tape - Only $29.95 (75 minutes)
Dr. Dallmann-Jones discusses how the Dysfunctional Family Survivor Syndrome impacts education. A must for educators!

Assessment forms:
Classification System for Child Abuse & Neglect (CSCAN)
Classification System for Abuse & Neglect in Adults (CSANA)
25 sheets per each 8.5 x 11 pad - Only $9.95
Each sheet includes all current CSCAN or CSANA categories in a checklist format. SPECIFY WHICH FORM YOU ARE ORDERING.

Note: All products fully guaranteed for the cost of the item(s).

ORDER FORM

Name_______________________________Tel____________
Address____
City&State___________________________Zip___________

___Copies of *Phoenix Flight Manual...Rising Above The Ashes of Ordinary Existence* @ $14.95 + $3 s/h = _______
___Copies of *Resolving Unfinished Business* @ $12.95 + $3 s/h = _______
___Stress Mgt. **Audio**-Tape @ $10.00 + $3 s/h = _______
___Self-Esteem **Video**-Tape @ $29.95 + $3 s/h = _______
___Dys. Fam. Surviv. **Video** @ $29.95 + $3 s/h = _______
___Dys. Fam. Classroom **Video** @ $29.95+$3s/h = _______
___CSCAN/CSANA Assess. pads@$9.95+$3s/h = _______

(Wisc. residents add 5% sales tax to mdse. price) _______
TOTAL: _________

(Allow 3 weeks for delivery. Satisfaction guaranteed for amount of purchase.)

Mail ORDER FORM along with check/money or purchase order #___________ to:

Three Blue Herons Publishing, Inc.
P. O. Box 463
Fond du Lac, WI 54936-0463
****

Resellers call 3BH for rates & terms: 414/921-6991

SPECIAL NOTE For Credit Card Holders:

You may place credit card orders of the *Phoenix Flight Manual* or *Resolving Unfinished Business* only. Call our distributor, Southern Publishers Group at: 1-800-628-0903 to place a credit card order for these two books. Other items listed must be ordered through 3BH.

~~~~~~

Accelerating Recovery
for Dysfunctional Family Survivors

"WINdows to the past opening DOORS to the future."

The WINDOORS Training & Program- The training is for those who wish to use our special field-tested method, The WINDOORS Program, in order to facilitate recovery for those suffering the DFS Syndrome. We train a person to not only complete their own unfinished business, but to help others do the same by conducting the 10-week WINDOORS Programs. The WINDOORS training is for anyone working with survivors of dysfunctional families, abuse & neglect, trauma, etc. Research over the past 6 years has shown that participants make quantum leaps in their recovery issues by participating in the WINDOORS Program.

This WINDOORS Training is a detailed and intense training that takes two years to complete, including two 10 day trainings on-site at Gillette Manor. (Cost includes books, materials, on-site instruction, and telephone consultations between trainings.) Call 414-921-0820 for further information.
~~~~~~

ABOUT THE AUTHOR

Anthony S. Dallmann-Jones, Ph.D.

Dr. Dallmann-Jones is currently a graduate professor of educational psychology at Marian College in Fond du Lac, Wisconsin. His master's degree is in research and testing, and his doctorate is in educational psychology. Both advanced degrees were earned at Florida State University in Tallahassee, Florida.

As a psychotherapist and former executive director of the National Association of Dysfunctional Family Survivors, Dr. Dallmann-Jones has conducted numerous trainings and seminars and given many addresses on the Dysfunctional Family Survivor Syndrome for schools, businesses and institutions across the United States and Canada.

Dr. Dallmann-Jones is author of several articles and tapes on survivorship, and is also the program designer, along with Dr. David Boers, of the Students At Risk (STARS) graduate curriculum at Marian College, the first of its kind in the United States.

Dr. Dallmann-Jones has authored many articles and several books:
STRATEGIES FOR TEACHING, Scarecrow Press, 1979.
THE EXPERT EDUCATOR, Three Blue Herons Publishing, 1994.
A HANDBOOK FOR EFFECTIVE TEACHING AND ASSESSMENT STRATEGIES, Twin Lights Publishing, 1995.
PHOENIX FLIGHT MANUAL...Rising Above The Ashes of Ordinary Existence, Three Blue Herons Publishing, 1995.

INDEX

12-step groups 94
abuse & neglect 8, 17, 25, 27, 29, 90, 92, 151
abuse . . 8, 9, 15, 17-29, 33, 37, 42, 55, 56, 61, 63, 69, 83-94, 97, 99-102, 104, 107-109, 111-121, 123, 125, 140, 142, 145-147, 150, 151
acceptance 32, 58, 59, 61, 74, 89, 134, 135
activation 8
adaptability 19, 20
adaptation 20, 21
addiction 20, 21, 33, 46, 49, 62, 71, 72, 75, 88, 113
adult emotional abuse 118
adult emotional self-abuse 118
adult financial abuse 121
adult financial self-abuse 121
adult mental abuse 116
adult mental self-abuse 116
adult physical abuse 114
adult physical self-abuse 113
adult sexual abuse 120
adult sexual self-abuse 119
American Self-Help Clearinghouse 94
anger 12, 20, 32, 33, 39, 40, 42, 47, 48, 58, 59, 70, 104
anxiety 20, 45, 69
assessment forms 109, 137, 151
avoiding emotions 32, 42, 44, 56, 72
breathing 4
bullying 42, 48, 105, 117

chemical dependency 103
Classification System of Child Abuse & Neglect 29
Compulsive Behaviors 35, 49, 65, 79-81, 113
Control Consciousness 31, 39, 51, 68
control . . . 20, 31, 32, 39-42, 51-53, 68-70, 72, 79, 83, 108, 128
co-alcoholic 126
co-dependence 20, 21, 146
Crisis Addiction 33, 46, 62, 75
CSANA 88, 109-111, 151, 152
CSCAN 1, 27, 88-90, 97, 99, 109, 110, 112, 151, 152
denial 3, 4, 31-33, 49, 52, 58, 60, 73, 74, 118, 125, 135
Drama Triangle 125, 128
drug addiction 21
dysfunctional family . 1-3, 8, 13-15, 21-24, 31-34, 37-39, 43, 45, 46, 48, 51, 64, 67, 74, 79, 94, 132, 150, 151, 154
Dysfunctional Family Survivor Syndrome 8, 13, 15, 23, 31, 38, 39, 51, 67, 150, 151, 154
education 9, 26, 38, 151
emotional abuse 87, 97, 102, 118, 140, 142
emotional neglect 103, 140, 142
emotions . . . 12, 31, 32, 42, 44, 56, 57, 60, 72-74, 87, 104, 118, 126, 128, 130, 132, 134, 135, 141, 143
emptiness 58, 59, 61
Family Health Continuum 140
family rules 42, 43
fear 20, 32, 33, 52, 56, 70, 104, 135
Gillette Manor 149
gossip 70
gratitude 32, 58-61, 74

grief work 44, 57, 60, 73, 74
grieving 60
Guessing at Normality 34, 47, 63, 76
Guilt from Overresponsibility 33, 61, 75
guilt 33, 40, 45, 58, 59, 61, 75, 125-127, 131, 133, 135
helplessness 41
Inability to Grieve 32, 33, 44, 57, 73
inertia 14
insanity 19
Institute for Transformational Studies 109, 149
intelligence 5, 18, 19, 149
intervention 4, 22, 29, 38, 67
Kamikaze kids 62
limits and boundaries 35,36, 54, 55, 63, 108
low self-esteem 34, 48, 63, 78, 118
lying 41, 102, 119
martyrdom 40
mental abuse 104, 116, 140, 142
mental neglect 106, 140, 142
mistrust 24, 53
modalities 53, 54
moderation 77
money addiction 71, 72
neglect . . . 1-4, 8, 9, 15, 17-22, 24-29, 37, 61, 63, 86, 88-92, 94, 97, 99, 100, 102, 103, 106, 108, 111, 112, 119, 123, 140, 142, 145, 150, 151
Nomenclature 25, 26, 89
normal 18, 22, 23, 34, 44, 47, 56, 63, 74, 76
Notation and Reporting System of Abuse & Neglect 90

numbness . . . 58, 74, 76
nurturing . . . 7, 17, 21, 31, 57, 103
overachieving . . . 55
overresponsibility . . . 33, 61, 75
Persecutor . . . 125, 127, 129, 131-133, 135
Personal Health Continuum . . . 137, 139, 142
PHOENIX FLIGHT MANUAL . . . 150, 152-154
Physical Abuse . . . 69, 91, 97, 99, 114, 140, 142
Physical Neglect . . . 100, 140, 142
PTSD . . . 42, 43
recovery . . . 7, 36, 37, 65, 146
reenactment . . . 18
RELATIONSHIPS . 34, 35, 38-40, 42, 68, 73, 86, 87, 93, 114, 125
Relationships of Abuse Forms . . . 86
Rescuer . . . 41, 125-129, 131, 133
sadness . . . 32, 33, 40, 47, 58, 59, 135
self-esteem . . . 21, 34, 48, 63, 64, 78, 79, 108, 118, 150, 152
self-pity . . . 126, 134
sensitivity . . . 17, 18, 84
Sexual Abuse . . . 86, 97, 100, 107, 115, 120, 140, 142, 147
Sexual Neglect . . . 108, 140, 142
shame . . . 24, 34, 41, 57, 86, 146, 147
shock . . . 32, 33, 58, 60
Spiritual Abuse . . . 28, 86
support groups . . . 37, 65, 94
suppression . . . 31, 73
survivors . . 1, 3, 9, 14, 22, 23, 28, 31-34, 39, 43, 44, 47, 48, 57, 67, 79, 147, 150, 154
susceptibility . . . 17

toolbox 7, 11, 12
trauma 8, 9, 22, 46, 146
Tunnel of Grief 32, 54, 57, 58, 74
underachieving 55
Vicarious Abuse 108, 140, 142
victim 41, 64, 87, 90, 92, 108, 125-128, 131, 133, 134
withholding 40, 103, 121
WINDOORS Program and Training 153
workaholism 71
WYSIWYG 22